MURDERS, MYSTERIES, AND MISDEMEANORS IN WASHINGTON STATE

Murders, Mysteries, and Misdemeanors in Washington State

Margaret LaPlante

AMERICA
THROUGH TIME®
ADDING COLOR TO AMERICAN HISTORY

Note: All photographs are courtesy of the Washington State Patrol.

America Through Time is an imprint of Fonthill Media LLC
www.through-time.com
office@through-time.com

Published by Arcadia Publishing by arrangement with Fonthill Media LLC
For all general information, please contact Arcadia Publishing:
Telephone: 843-853-2070
Fax: 843-853-0044
E-mail: sales@arcadiapublishing.com
For customer service and orders:
Toll-Free 1-888-313-2665

www.arcadiapublishing.com

First published 2023

ISBN 978-1-63499-466-8

Typeset in 10.5pt on13pt Sabon
Printed and bound in England

CONTENTS

INTRODUCTION

Nestled between the ocean and the mountains of Washington state lie true crime murders, mysteries, and misdemeanors.

"You can't kill thirteen people unintentionally," argued a prosecuting attorney during a murder trial. "I cannot annihilate the whole town of Tacoma to keep your big mouth shut. I hope you learned something," warned a man who was later convicted of three murders. "These ballpoint pens are dangerous," said a convicted murderer after freeing himself from handcuffs and leg irons using such a pen. Minutes later, he used the restraints to chain two police officers to a tree before fleeing in their police car. "The children went to sleep real easy. Better call the cops," were the words spoken by a man when his girlfriend returned home, moments before she discovered he had murdered her children. "An amazing series of mistaken identity," said a man accused of several attacks on women, all the while claiming he was not involved. "Don't give me any trouble, I just killed a man five minutes ago," was the warning given to a business owner moments before he was taken hostage by the armed suspect. "It would be difficult for a mind to make up a more sordid train of events," argued a prosecuting attorney when describing a one-day crime spree in Camas that included a homicide, an armed robbery, an auto theft, a double kidnapping, and a shootout with the police at a roadblock. "I am not a safe person to be at large," said a man dubbed the "phantom sniper of Detroit, Michigan," before he moved to Washington state and committed yet another murder. "If I had it to do over again, I would kill my wife," uttered a man on trial for murder. "I'm a dead duck. When you kill a cop, you're through," stated a man convicted of killing a police sergeant. "About the most rugged case I have ever seen," reported a law enforcement official in describing a brutal murder in 1950 that later brought foreign dignitaries half way around the globe to assist with the murder trial.

I
THE FLY-IN-KILLER

"He has no sense of value to his own life and therefore relates no value to any other human life," reported Portland psychiatrist Dr. Wendell Hutchens in 1965. He was describing John Anderson who became known as the "Fly-In-Killer."

John was born on May 6, 1945. He grew up in Riverside, California. He sailed through school without any problems and enrolled at Riverside Community College. John learned to fly while attending community college. In addition to taking classes, John worked two part-time jobs. He was employed as a darkroom technician for the *Riverside Press-Enterprise* in their photography department and as a salesperson at a local camera store. He also did freelance photography work on the side.

In 1965, John was enrolled at Pepperdine College in Los Angeles where he was pursuing a degree in photojournalism. On July 9, 1965, John drove to a small airport in Hawthorne, California. He rented a single-engined airplane, explaining that he needed to fly to Riverside to visit his parents. In actuality, he planned to fly to Alaska. He placed a duffel bag with three firearms in the airplane and took off.

That evening, John landed at Pearson Air Park in Vancouver, Washington, and was granted permission to leave the airplane overnight. He told the employee at the airport he planned to stay in Vancouver for a month for a photography assignment. The employee gave John a ride to a motel in downtown Vancouver where John registered using his own name but gave a fictitious address in San Diego.

The following afternoon, John returned to Pearson Air Park and asked the employees to refuel the airplane. While waiting for the airplane, John called for a taxicab. Genevieve Jennings responded to the call, driving her City Cab Ford sedan. Genevieve drove John to two pawn shops where he tried to pawn one of his firearms. The first pawn shop told John they did not purchase firearms; the other turned him away because he was not twenty-one years old.

John asked Genevieve to drive him back to Pearson Air Park. Just as they pulled into the air park, John turned the firearm on Genevieve and pulled the trigger twice. He pushed Genevieve out of the still-moving vehicle. John got behind the wheel of the taxicab and fled out of the air park, driving at speeds up to 100 mph.

Genevieve was rushed to a hospital but died hours later from the two gunshot wounds. Police bulletins were sent out via teletype machines throughout the region seeking John and the City Cab Ford sedan. The Washington State Patrol was joined by officers from the Vancouver Police Department, Battle Ground Police Department, Clark County Sheriff's Department, and reserve deputies who were on duty at Amboy's Territorial Days.

As John drove erratically through Battle Ground, a marshal by the name of Hal Huffstutler spotted the taxicab and gave chase. Some 6 miles later, John failed to negotiate a 90-degree turn. In the small town of Duluth, west of Battle Ground, John crashed into a small barber shop. He immediately jumped out of the taxicab and ran into the barber shop with the loaded firearm. As he entered the building, he opened fire, shooting Dennis Jones, who was getting a haircut. Another customer, Edgar Waser, age twenty-three, was shot twice. The barber, Howard Morford, age sixty, attempted to push John out of the building, but as he did so, John fired twice, hitting Howard in the back and the side. Howard died just as the police arrived on scene. For the next fifteen minutes, John held the police at bay before surrendering. John was arrested and booked into the Clark County jail.

Dennis and Edgar survived the gunshots. Services were held for Howard and Genevieve. Howard was survived by his wife, his adult son, four grandchildren, and two brothers. Genevieve and her husband operated the City Cab company together. She was survived by her parents, her husband, a brother, four sisters, two sons, a daughter, and eight grandchildren.

A reporter with the Associated Press spoke to John's parents. His father told the reporter that other than some traffic infractions, John had never been in trouble with the law. John's parents were shocked to learn that John had rented an airplane and left California. They thought he was at college attending summer classes. John's father described his son as a "gentle, well-behaved boy." He added, "I'm biased, I suppose, but this is my assessment of him." John's father went onto say, "He's never been in any serious trouble. I have no idea of what might have happened. I certainly don't care to speculate. I'm in no emotional position to hazard a guess."[1]

John's former manager at the *Riverside Press-Enterprise* newspaper told reporter Neil Modie with *The Columbian*, that John was "an excellent photographer" and "the hardest-working guy I ever knew." He mentioned John owned expensive camera equipment and had a gun that he used for hunting.

John sent for his textbooks and spent most of his time studying in his jail cell. John underwent psychiatric testing prior to entering a plea of guilty of second-degree murder for Howard Morton. He received a sentence of life imprisonment. The State Parole Board set John's minimum sentence at thirty-five years, with the understanding that with good behavior his sentence could be reduced to twenty-three years and four months.

John's parents watched from a distance as their son was led in handcuffs and leg irons from the Clark County jail to a waiting station wagon to transport him to the Walla Walla prison where John became inmate No. 125278. He spent eight years at Walla Walla prison awaiting his sentence for the murder of Genevieve. Finally, in 1974, he was returned to the Clark County courthouse. John pled guilty to a charge of second-degree murder for Genevieve Jennings. He received a concurrent life sentence. The following year, John was granted a training release to attend the University of Washington, but it would not be the last the public heard from him.

On January 13, 1980, restaurant manager Harry Gee came out of his kitchen at the South China Doll Restaurant in south King County. Harry was carrying a food order but dropped it immediately when he saw a masked man robbing his cashier. He gave chase out to the parking lot and was able to pull the mask off the robber. Just as he did so, the robber turned and fired three times, hitting Harry. Before the robber fled, he shot Harry two more times point blank. The robber got in his getaway car and fled the scene before law enforcement arrived. A witness heard the killer say to the getaway driver, "I hope the son of a bitch is dead." Harry died from his gunshot wounds.

As detectives with the King County Sheriff's Office began their investigation into the murder at the South China Doll Restaurant, they were bothered by the similarities to another restaurant shooting wherein an unknown suspect opened fire at the Yorktown Restaurant in Lakewood. The shooter fired eight rounds, striking six people, which resulted in three deaths and three injuries. The shooting became known as the Yorktown Massacre.

Two months after Harry was murdered, John and his associate, Robert Ross Stratton, age forty-three, were arrested for the murder of Harry Gee. The investigation revealed that Robert was the getaway driver and John was responsible for the robbery and murder. John was charged with one count of first-degree murder and one count of first-degree robbery. At the time John was arrested, the police believed he was responsible for other robberies in King County and they charged him with those robberies as well. Robert was charged with first-degree robbery, being a felon in possession of a firearm, and rendering criminal assistance in an armed robbery which resulted in death.

Months later, John went on trial in Superior Court Judge William Goodloe's courtroom. After a short trial, the jury returned a verdict of guilty of first-degree murder and guilty of six counts of first-degree robbery. Judge Goodloe handed down a sentence of life in prison plus twenty years for the murder. He sentenced John to twenty years for five of the robberies, and ten years for the other robbery. The terms for the robberies were to run consecutive to the murder term. During the sentencing, Judge Goodloe stressed to John, "I will recommend to the parole board that you never be paroled."

Robert was convicted of rendering criminal assistance in an armed robbery that resulted in death. He was sentenced to one year in the King County jail with a five-year suspended prison sentence and five years' probation. As Robert was counting down the days until his freedom, Detective Commander Richard Minshull and Detective Jim Flint with the Olympia Police Department were working on the case of the murder of U.S. Army Sergeant Jesus Hernandez, age thirty-eight. On February 19, 1979, Jesus was shot as he was leaving the Vips Restaurant with his estranged wife, Joyce, age thirty-seven.

While the detectives with the Olympia Police Department were working on Jesus' murder and detectives with the King County Sheriff's Office were working on the homicide of Harry Gee; detectives with the Pierce County Sheriff's Office were still trying to solve the Yorktown Massacre that took place on December 18, 1979. As the investigation continued, they noticed a common thread among the cases. They determined that John was the shooter in the Yorktown Massacre and that Robert and Joyce were involved.

The investigators were able to piece together a murder for hire plot. Robert was charged with first-degree murder and Joyce was charged with first-degree manslaughter. Joyce pled guilty to one count of manslaughter for the murder of her estranged husband, Jesus. She admitted to agreeing to pay Robert $15,000 to kill Jesus. Judge Gerry Alexander sentenced Joyce to a maximum of ten years in prison. In exchange, Joyce agreed to testify against Robert. Initially there was a misunderstanding about her sentence with Joyce expecting to only serve one year in jail. When she learned she was heading to prison, she revoked her willingness to testify at Robert's upcoming trial. After some reflection Joyce decided to testify so that Robert would not be "free and out on the streets."

As the pieces of the puzzle came together, the detectives were able to determine when Joyce hired Robert to murder Jesus, they were in a relationship. When that relationship ended, Joyce allegedly told her new boyfriend, Jim Hall, about the murder for hire plot. Jim worked as a bartender at the Yorktown Restaurant. Robert and John decided to shoot up the Yorktown Restaurant in an effort to scare Joyce so she would not tell anyone else about the murder. They reasoned that Joyce's boyfriend would die in the shooting, thus preventing him from telling anyone about Jesus' murder.

Robert's trial opened to a packed courtroom. Extra security measures were put into place, including covering the windows of the courtroom to prevent a sniper from attempting to murder Robert. All visitors to the courthouse were subjected to a pat-down search for any hidden weapons. Numerous police officers dressed in plain clothes were placed strategically throughout the courthouse.

People came from near and far to observe the trial. One woman told the media that her mother was visiting from Idaho and they chose to come to the courthouse to view the trial. This was in comparison to their previous year's visit when they visited Mount St. Helens as it was erupting. One woman brought her embroidery project and worked on it while listening to the testimony; others took copious notes.

Larry White, age forty-two, took the witness stand and told the seven women and five men of the jury that he was approached by John to participate in the murder for hire, to which he declined. He explained he later moved in with Robert, Robert's girlfriend, and another roommate. He went on to say that soon after he moved in, John also moved in.

Larry told the panel of jurists that on the night of the Yorktown Massacre, John asked him to "help him do something." It was Larry's testimony that he turned down the request, and instead stayed home and watched television. He recalled John left the house carrying a blue bag that he knew contained ski masks, gloves, firearms, ammunition, and tape.

Larry said he was watching television later that night, when a news report came on stating there had been a shooting at the Yorktown Restaurant. He told the jury that John returned home shortly after the news report. He recalled that John was agitated. He said John turned on a police scanner and "glued his ear to it." As Larry continued his testimony, he said Robert later told him John was a "cold-blooded killer who just stood in there and popped them off."

Joyce took the witness stand and immediately implicated Robert in the plot to murder her estranged husband, Jesus. Joyce referred to Robert as a "hitman." She admitted they had been in a relationship prior to Jesus' murder. She told the jury after they broke off their relationship, she left town without providing a forwarding address because she was afraid that he would find her.

Joyce told the jury after she moved, she met Jesus and they married in 1978 when he was stationed at Fort Lewis. She said everything was fine in the beginning, but then Jesus began drinking and would frequently beat her.

Joyce said they had not been married very long when she ran into Robert at a tavern in Olympia. They talked that night at the bar and soon after they began having an affair. She recalled that Robert kept asking her to insure her jewelry, which was valued at $30,000. She explained he wanted her to file an insurance claim and split the profits with him. She told the jury that she never followed through with insuring her jewelry.

Joyce admitted she told Robert about the difficulties she was having with her marriage, citing Jesus' drinking and assaulting her. "We talked hypothetically. I said what if I wanted my husband killed. He said if you wanted your husband killed, it would cost $5,000 before and $5,000 after."[2]

Robert, she said, gave her a deadline of two weeks to come up with the first $5,000. When they met two weeks later, Joyce said she told Robert she was not able to come up with the money, and that she had changed her mind. Joyce told the court that Robert informed her it was too late to back out. She said Robert told her he had already paid an attorney $3,000 to "work out the details and legalities. He said it would be $15,000 instead of $10,000 and I would pay him when I collected from [the] Army life insurance."[3]

Joyce admitted she and Robert were in an intimate relationship when Jesus was murdered. Joyce described for the jury, the night her estranged husband was killed. The plan, she said, was she and Jesus would leave the Vips Restaurant at the same time as other people left, so it would look as though Jesus' murder was a random killing. Robert had already told her he planned to use a .22-caliber rifle and shoot from a pile of debris nearby. Joyce's testimony was that Robert planned to shoot "a bunch of people so the police would not know where to start looking. He said we'll have to shoot you to make it look good. I was hoping he was teasing but I was nervous."

Joyce admitted she met Jesus at a tavern in south Tacoma prior to going to the Vips Restaurant. She said they left the restaurant and headed out to the parking lot:

> My husband opened the door and put one foot up. I heard a noise and
> he just fell. I called his name a couple of times and there was no answer. I

got out of the van and he was just lying there. I just stood and looked at him for a minute.[4]

She said she was surprised she did not hear a gunshot. Joyce added that she never saw anyone leave the area.

As Joyce continued to testify, she told of the difficulty she had trying to collect on Jesus' life insurance policy. She said she met with an attorney who "seemed to know all about" Jesus' death. She went onto say that the attorney gave her his business card in the event the police ever considered her a suspect in Jesus' murder. Joyce explained that she did eventually receive a check from the insurance company, but it was made payable to her and the attorney. Joyce testified she received $27,000 from Jesus' life insurance, $28,000 from the sale of their house, and $4,800 from selling Jesus' van. From those proceeds, she admitted she gave $5,800 to Robert.

Special Prosecutor Edward Schaller, Jr., asked Joyce about the Yorktown Massacre. She said at the time of the shooting, she was no longer dating Robert; but instead had a new boyfriend, Jim Hall. She explained she was in the restaurant the night of the shooting with her mother and her mother's boyfriend. Joyce explained to the jury that Jim was working as the bartender that night.

Joyce described the actual shooting saying:

> Then the back door opened and a man stepped in. He had a ski mask on. At first I just looked up and saw him. The customers there are always clowning around, and I just thought it was someone trying to be funny. But it wasn't funny when he started firing.[5]

She said the shooter fired in the direction of the bar, but missed Jim because minutes before he had left the bar and joined her at a table. However, her mother's boyfriend was one of the six victims who were shot. Joyce said her mother's boyfriend survived, along with two other men, but three men died from being shot.

Joyce told the jury she was sure Robert was responsible for the shooting because she still owed him money for the contract killing and she knew he was angry that she told Jim about Jesus' murder. When questioned by Prosecutor Schaller, Joyce explained, "I knew it wasn't Stratton [who did the actual shooting.] He [the shooter] wasn't large enough. I thought it was Anderson. They [the shooter and John Anderson] were the same size."[6]

Joyce told the court the morning after the shooting, she called Robert and he stopped by her house. It was at that time he told her, "I cannot annihilate the whole town of Tacoma to keep your big mouth shut. I hope you learned something," referring to the motive behind the shooting. "I told him my mother's boyfriend was shot. He said he was sorry. He said Jim Hall was the luckiest SOB because he was not behind the bar at the time of the shooting."[7]

Joyce said the shooting weighed heavy on her mind for months before she contacted an attorney and asked for legal help with notifying law enforcement. She told the jury about the plea agreement she accepted in exchange for testifying against her former boyfriend. She spoke of visiting Robert soon after he was arrested. She said he held a note up to the window in the visiting room asking her to give his mother $4,200. Joyce said she nodded in agreement to his request. He then held up a second note, letting her know that he loved her.

Under cross-examination by Robert's defense attorney, John Jarrett, Joyce admitted she initially lied to Detective Walt Stout when he questioned everyone who was at the Yorktown Restaurant on the night of the shooting. Joyce admitted, "I don't remember everything I told him, but I know I didn't want to tell him the truth." Upon further cross-examination, Joyce admitted she assured Robert's mother "not to worry" because she was "going to get amnesia," adding, "you and I both know Bob is not guilty." On the witness stand, Joyce explained she only said that because she assumed law enforcement had bugged their telephones. She quickly added, "The truth was that her and I both knew Bob was guilty."

It was Joyce's testimony that the year before the murders, Robert was involved with the murder of his mother's husband. According to Joyce, this took place during an apparent robbery. She went on to say that same year, 1978, she and Robert were at a restaurant in Seattle when a man asked to speak to Robert. She said they left together but Robert returned a short time later alone and told her he had slit the man's throat and placed the body in a dumpster. Before Joyce completed her four days of testimony, she told the jury that the attorney who helped her successfully claim Jesus' life insurance was providing Robert with contract killings.

Robert's defense attorney accused Joyce of "juicing up her story." She adamantly denied doing so and reiterated that she was telling the truth.

A former roommate of Robert's, Dorothy Pulliam took the witness stand. It was her testimony that Robert lived with her and her children from 1978 to 1979. Dorothy recalled Robert being very anxious the night Jesus was murdered. Dorothy told the jury he went to Aberdeen to visit John, and afterwards he was much calmer. However, she did remember having a dispute with Robert while the two of them were at the Vips Restaurant later that year. According to Dorothy, Robert said he would "blow my brains out too."

Dorothy informed the panel of jurists that Robert owned a bar in Seattle that burned to the ground while he was living with her. She testified that on the night of the fire, Robert closed the bar four hours early. Dorothy said one of the bar's employees who usually slept in the bar spent the night at her house instead. She recalled a phone call came in at approximately 2 a.m. informing Robert that his business was on fire. Dorothy testified that upon learning the news, Robert "just rolled over and went to sleep, as if nothing had happened." Dorothy confirmed an investigation into the cause of the fire was conducted, but no criminal charges were ever filed.

A former co-worker of John's told the jury he recalled Robert stopped by the auto dealership where they worked the day after Jesus was murdered.

Those who secured a seat in the packed courtroom were not disappointed the day Robert strode to the witness stand. He admitted to having an affair with Joyce while she was still married to Jesus. He denied having anything to do with the murder; instead, he pinned the blame on Joyce. His attorney then asked, "What did you say when Joyce told you she was involved in her husband's death?" Robert did not miss a beat, before replying, "I thought about it awhile and then I told her she'd better keep her mouth shut." When asked further details about Joyce's alleged involvement in Jesus' death, Robert implied his life would be in danger if he answered the question. "It would be hazardous to my health. I don't want to be shot."

"She's deranged," was Robert's explanation as to why Joyce would swear under oath that he murdered her estranged husband. After Robert told the jury, he was only interested in Joyce for her money, the prosecution asked, "You fancy yourself as a lady's man, don't you?" Robert simply replied, "I manage to get by."

The prosecution asked about Robert's feelings towards Dorothy who previously testified. Robert categorized her as "confused in most of her testimony." Robert described another former girlfriend who testified against him as a bitter, vindictive woman who hated him because he left her for someone else.

Special Prosecutor Schaller asked Robert if he was an alcoholic after he spoke of spending most evenings in local bars and taverns. His response was "probably." When asked how he made a living, Robert replied, "I play poker a lot and work for myself." That answer brought out the question, "You work for yourself doing what?" Robert simply stated, "Playing poker." Special Prosecutor Schaller probed further asking, "You mean that's your sole income?" Robert quickly replied, "I would say so."

The prosecution's cross-examination of Robert took a turn when Robert suddenly asked, "Am I on trial here for my attitude Mr. Schaller?"

The prosecution quickly fired back, "I'm asking the questions here—and yes, you may be, to a certain extent, Mr. Stratton."

The next line of questioning had to do with Robert's criminal record. He admitted to serving time in the Washington State Penitentiary for first-degree burglary, three counts of second-degree assault, and robbery. He explained he had also been in trouble with the law for rendering criminal assistance to persons who committed a robbery and first-degree murder, and concealing them. This charge stemmed from the murder of Harry Gee. Robert stressed to the jury that he did not have anything to do with his stepfather's murder. He quickly added that two men were convicted of murdering his stepfather. He emphatically stated he never slit the throat of a man and placed his body in a dumpster. When asked why he thought Joyce would say such a thing, Robert replied, "Same sick mind that came up with the rest of this garbage."

Robert admitted Joyce bought him a suit, watch, jewelry, and a camera when she received the proceeds from Jesus' life insurance. He was asked if she ever gave him money, alluding to the $15,000 she said she paid Robert to murder Jesus. Robert quickly replied, "No such luck." However, he added, "as long as there are women out there, I will never have to murder for money."

Robert provided the jury with his alibi the night the shooting took place. He explained he and a friend were in Ocean Shores looking at a boat that was for sale. His friend took the witness stand and corroborated Robert's alibi.

Ray Davis took the stand and explained his job as a crime reconstructionist. He told the court, based on his research, that the person who murdered Jesus was parked in a vehicle behind Jesus' van. He concluded Joyce could not have pulled the trigger based on where she said she was when Jesus was shot. Ray said he was not able to determine if a shotgun or a rifle was used.

After four weeks of testimony, the jury received the case and began deliberations. It only took them two hours to reach a verdict of guilty of first-degree murder for the contract killing of Jesus. Robert was sentenced to life imprisonment.

One day shy of the second anniversary of the Yorktown Restaurant, Robert and John were charged with three counts of first-degree murder and three counts of first-degree assault. They each pled innocent to all charges. Robert and John were facing a term of life in prison, as the state of Washington did not have the death penalty in place when the shooting took place. The three men who were murdered were Donald Williams, age forty-one, Robert Casses, age fifty-one, and Steve Allen, age thirty-seven.

In April 1982, a decision was made to try Robert and John together, over the objection of the defense who argued that neither would receive a fair trial. Pierce County Superior Court Judge Waldo Stone presided over the dual trial. Chief Criminal Deputy Prosecutor Ellsworth Connelly represented the state of Washington. John was represented by David Murdach. Robert was represented by Jerry Horne. The jury was divided equally between men and women.

Some of the first to testify were patrons of the restaurant on the night of the shooting. They spoke of rendering aid to the men struck by bullets prior to first responders arriving on scene. None of the witnesses were able to describe the shooter, who wore a ski mask and dark clothing.

The prosecution explained that some people who participate in target shooting mark their bullets. He explained that the police located a bullet with what appeared to be red nail polish in front of a restaurant in Seattle following a robbery. In King County, they located similar bullets with red nail polish outside of the South China Restaurant where Harry Gee was killed. At the Yorktown Restaurant, the prosecution explained, investigators found eight bullets with what appeared to be red nail polish.

Larry White took the witness stand as he promised to do in exchange for not being prosecuted for his knowledge of the crime. He told the jury that on the night of the shooting, he watched as John left the house carrying a duffel bag that Larry recognized as the bag they used while committing other robberies. He expanded by saying inside the bag were guns, ski masks, gloves, and other essential items for committing crimes. Larry told the panel of jurists that when John returned home, he was "very agitated, upset, tense." He recalled that John immediately turned on their police scanner and began listening to it. Larry said the following day he overheard Robert telling John he "really impressed her." Days later he asked Robert about the Yorktown Restaurant shooting. "He told me it was a demonstration to prove a point," before adding, "John just stood there and popped them off, like he was on a shooting range." Larry told the jury that Robert had taken John to the restaurant days earlier to "case the layout." Before Larry stepped down from the witness stand, he admitted he had an extensive criminal record dating back to 1957.

The defense team told the jury that Larry's story was an attempt to save his own self from the pending prosecution for twelve robberies he was charged with. The defense expanded on their theory by saying the deputies used Larry's story to pressure Joyce into saying the duo was responsible for the Yorktown Massacre. Both John and Robert used their time on the witness stand to accuse the other of being responsible for the mass murders.

For the fourth time in his life, John was convicted of first-degree murder when the jury returned a guilty verdict. He was thirty-seven years old at the time the jury found both he and Robert guilty of the Yorktown

Massacre. John, with an IQ of 138, had spent more time in prison than as a free man. Both defense attorneys declared they would appeal the verdict. Judge Stone sentenced both men to three consecutive life terms in prison. At the time of the sentencing, they were both already serving life terms for other murders.

Robert's sentence was upheld by the State Court of Appeals. However, John's sentence was overturned by the Court of Appeals. It was their belief the court erred by allowing Larry to testify about what Robert told him regarding the shooting at the restaurant. Two years later, the Washington Supreme Court upheld John's conviction of the restaurant murders.

2
THE FLOATERS FLEET

They became known as the "floaters fleet" but they were actually homicide victims that began appearing in 1907 in the river near Aberdeen.

Some of the bodies were seen floating down the waterfront but the current prevented anyone from retrieving the bodies. Of the bodies the authorities were able to recover, they were able to determine that the cause of death for some was a gunshot wound. The advanced state of decomposition made identifying most of the bodies impossible. Still others were not known to anyone and were never identified.

At first, the bodies were thought to be men who fell overboard and drowned. But as the body count continued, Aberdeen, with an estimated population of 12,000 people, got the reputation as the "Wild West" as more people began to look at the saloons as the culprit. They blamed the homicides on drunken brawls and fights at the local taverns.

The owners of taverns in and around Aberdeen became increasingly tired of being blamed for the floaters fleet. They felt the accusation was unjust and decided to investigate the matter. Patrick McHugh took the lead in the investigation. At the time, he owned the Paddy McHugh tavern on the Aberdeen waterfront.

Patrick was good friends with William "Billy" Gohl. Billy worked as an agent for the Aberdeen Sailors' Union. Billy became an outspoken critic of those who had been put in charge of the investigation into the corpses floating in the river. He felt the authorities had not done enough to determine how these men had met their fate.

The community of tavern owners and workers were well acquainted with the local sailors. The rumor mill frequently mentioned that Billy was somehow involved with the murders, but nothing concrete was ever established. That is until 1910 when a citizen told the mayor of Aberdeen he knew "enough about Billy Gohl to send him to the gallows." The anonymous citizen informed Mayor Benn that Billy was responsible for the floaters fleet. The person explained Billy had a trap door in his office that went directly into the water. The mayor was told that when Billy was alone with a sailor, he would murder the sailor and drop the dead body down the trap door into the water. Mayor Benn and the police chief of Aberdeen, George Dunn, began their own investigation, which led them to John Klingenberg, age thirty-two.

John quickly confessed to murdering one of the victims by the name of Charles Henry Hadberg. But just as quickly, he placed the blame squarely on Billy, saying his own life would have been in danger had he not killed Charles. He also confessed that he and Billy murdered John Hoffman and tied an anchor around his body before dropping him in the water from Billy's boat. Both murders, he explained, took place in December 1909.

Police Chief Dunn located Billy and placed him under arrest. Chief Dunn referred to Billy as "The Ghoul of Grays Harbor:"

> Forty men are known to have been murdered on Grays Harbor in recent years. I believe that William Gohl was the prime mover in many times 40 murders, many of which have never come to light, for most of the men whom Gohl murdered never floated. Their bones lie buried in the mud at the bottom of the harbor...[1]

Six months after Billy's arrest, the trial got underway with Judge Ben Sheek presiding. A crowd estimated to be 600 filled the courtroom to capacity, with an overflow crowd outside. The jury learned Billy had been accused of murder while living in Germany. He fled to Australia, but was soon in trouble with the law there. He then came to America and lived for a time in California before arriving in Aberdeen with his wife in 1903.

The jury was told that in 1905, Billy allegedly asked his friends to join him in removing a crew from a non-union schooner named *Fearless*. Billy knew the name of one of the crew members. He and his friends went by boat and pulled up next to the schooner. They were invited on board after Billy asked to see his friend. Billy and his friends attempted to unarm the men on board *Fearless*. Before they could finish taking the guns from the crew, shots rang out on both sides. An estimated 150 shots were fired. At least one man was killed in the gunfight. Billy was convicted of piracy. The Sailor's Union paid his $1,200 fine. The jury was allowed to view the bullet-riddled ship from 1905.

John Klingenberg took the witness stand. He told the court he was from Denmark, but came to Grays Harbor seven years prior to the murder. He explained he had been working on the schooner *A.J. West* as recent as

1909. John was asked where he was staying at the time of the murder. He replied, "In a cabin about 100 yards from Billy Gohl's place. On December 20 was working as donkey engineer on boat. I saw Mr. Gohl that evening up at Sailor's union hall." When John was asked what happened next, he explained:

> A friend of his, Waldemar Nelson, came to the boat and told me Billy Gohl wanted to see me. I went up there later on. First he took me into another room and got his overcoat. He got two guns, one automatic and one hammerless, and handed me one. He said "here take that." I took one and all three of us went downstairs. We shook Nelson because Billy Gohl said Nelson "acted so childish when he had to handle a gun."[2]

John said he suggested that Billy patch things up with Charles, but was quickly rebuffed. He continued:

> Next day I went to work and come ashore about 7 o'clock that night. I met Billy Gohl and John Hoffman outside the union hall. Gohl hailed me and said, "Are you ready Johnny" and I said yes. He told Hoffman and me to wait there a few minutes and he would be back. I waited, although I didn't care much about going down the bay because Billy Gohl said he was going to kill Hadberg and I didn't feel good about it.[3]

Judge Sheeks did not allow any reference to the murder of John Hoffman during John's testimony. He did, however, allow Prosecutor Campbell to question John regarding guns being fired on the boat ride from Aberdeen to Indian Creek. John testified that Billy fired four or five shots from an automatic .38-caliber revolver.

As they traveled by boat, John said, Billy gave him orders to kill Charles, adding, "don't take him until after we get off the mud flat." John told the court that upon reaching Charles' location, "Hadberg must have heard us coming, for he came out and said, 'You ought to have seen what a lot of fun I had here a while ago. I shot a deer.'" Billy, he said, quickly replied, "That's nothing. You ought to see the fun we had just a while ago," referring to the shots fired.

John spoke about how they spent the rest of the evening after they met up with Charles:

> I had a bottle of whiskey and when we got out of the launch I gave Charley Hadberg a drink. Charley Hadberg offered to carry me across the mud on his back, but I refused. We all three went into Charley Hadberg's shack and had some lunch, some soup or mulligan, or

something. I couldn't eat, so I excused myself. Billy Gohl talked to Charley Hadberg and told him he had a sloop lying in the mud up the bay and wanted Charley Hadberg to help us get it off. After a while Billy Gohl said we would sleep there and go back [the] next morning. Charley Hadberg gave Billy Gohl Hoffman's bed to sleep in and Hadberg gave me his bed to sleep in.[4]

John told the packed courtroom he was unable to sleep, adding:

I didn't have the nerve I ought to have had, because I knew what I had to do. In the morning early I went down and got the launch out of the slough and brought it up to the shack. When I came up Billy Gohl and Hadberg were standing there.[5]

John went on to explain that Charles offered them a large anchor:

After Hadberg threw the anchor aboard Billy Gohl tried to make the engine work. I was in the cabin and Billy Gohl said to me, "You take him or I'm going to take him—there is only one thing you've got to do—pull the trigger four or five times, but don't shoot him [Hadberg] until we get out of the slough; be quick, because he's got a gun on him. I will give you the sign."

He went out after saying that and told Hadberg it would take too long to get the engines to work and ordered us to pull back up the bay with our oars. We were pulling away at the oars and I couldn't look at the man, although he was right in front of me, because I knew what was going to come. Gohl came in at that minute but I couldn't get no shot then. Billy Gohl says to Hadberg, "Why don't you turn around; you'll pull better." I said, "Let the man sit there."

Right then Hadberg looked around at us and asked Gohl if he couldn't fix the engines. "Yes, I'll fix 'em all right," said Gohl, and he pushed me in the back and said, "Now take him," and I fired; it was two or three, I don't know. I was so excited that I lifted the man on the gunwales and was going to throw him overboard right then and there. Gohl stopped me and said, "Hold on, we are going to tie him up to this anchor." We did so. I helped him lash the rope around Hadberg's shoulders to the anchor, and the body was thrown into the water.[6]

John told the jury that for the next minute or two he thought Billy was going to shoot him, as he still had his gun out. Instead, he explained, Billy told him to throw his gun in the water, and he did the same. They then washed out the blood in the boat. John explained that Billy told him if anyone asked, to say Charles went to Alaska. He admitted he received, "a piece of money from Gohl" and the promise of a new suit and gun.

Aberdeen Police Constable George Dean explained to the jury how he located Charles' body:

> Indian Creek which empties into South Bay, about four miles from Aberdeen, is a small creek, perhaps 20 feet wide. Yesterday, February 1st, we went down the bay in a small boat and entered the creek at nearly low water. About a half-mile from the shore we found the body of Hadberg, lying in the creek. Gohl had mistaken the depth of the water at low tide—the body was in plain view, and we did not have to drag for it.
>
> On the back of the corpse was a 50-pound anchor, sufficient to hold the body down. It had been placed there with care. An examination showed two bullet wounds in the head. By the side of the body, also weighted down, we found three guns, with one of which we believe Hadberg was murdered. No other evidence was found.[7]

Constable Dean described for the jury how nine men in rowboats dragged the water but were unable to locate the body of John Hoffman.

The next witness was Richard Miles, who identified the satchel of tools and three weapons brought up from the riverbed. Next, Emil Olsen took the witness stand and identified Charles by a piece of skin covered with a tattoo that had been removed from his body at the morgue.

The jury heard from several witnesses who testified to hearing a man scream from the water and hearing gunshots. Patrick McHugh took the stand and told the jury that Billy told him, "Well, we landed those fellows last night. Hoffman was pretty tough. Klingenberg was with me. We went down to Indian Creel and took Hadberg. We put him on a big anchor for a pillow in the bay."

The jury learned during a longshoremen's strike in 1906, Billy threatened to murder the mayor and other officials in Aberdeen, all the while claiming he had murdered before. When fires broke out in the homes of people opposed to his ideas, he became the primary suspect, but was never officially charged with any crimes. The strike ended and work began again.

It was Billy, the jury learned, who identified some of the "floaters fleet." As a union representative, Billy had contact with many of the men who later turned up dead. Part of his job was to cash payroll checks and assist the sailors with any needs they had while they were on land. Billy also held their money when they were out at sea for a period of time. The police investigation revealed that not one of the murder victims had any money left in his account that Billy managed. Most of the bodies were buried in the pauper's area of the cemetery.

The jury learned one hasty identification cast suspicion on Billy. One of the bodies still had a watch on the wrist. The man had been shot in the head. Constable Dean asked Billy if he could identify the body. He quickly uttered the name, "Otto Kurtz of Germany." Despite the identification by Billy, the constable decided to investigate the matter further. He went to the boarding house where the man had recently lived. There, he saw not only a photograph of the man, but also mail addressed to the man with the name Rudolph Alterman. Further investigation revealed inside the watch was the name of the watchmaker—Otto Kurtz. Nothing came of the investigation, but the police were wary of allowing Billy to identify any more bodies.

After nine days of testimony, the case was handed off to the jury to begin deliberations. It did not take them long to return a verdict of guilty. Billy was sentenced to life imprisonment. In total, he served nineteen years between the Walla Walla prison and later the state mental hospital, where he died in 1929. John Klingenberg was sentenced to fifteen years for his role in the murder of Charles Hadberg.

3
BONNIE AND FRED WELCH

When Carol Welch returned to her home in Vancouver on December 11, 1964, her roommate informed her, "The children went to sleep real easy. Better call the cops." Carol's roommate quickly left the house leaving her to find her daughter Bonnie Lee, age seventeen, and her son, Fred Edward, age sixteen, murdered in their beds. Nine-year-old Renee was asleep in the upstairs portion of the house and had not been harmed. Carol's youngest child, Sherrie, age two, was at a relative's house.

Carol's roommate, John William Hawkins, age twenty-five, had been released from a New Mexico prison two months prior to the murders. He was sent to prison in 1959 in New Mexico for larceny, illegal entry, and contributing to the delinquency of a minor. He was paroled in 1961, but re-arrested the following year for violating the terms of his parole. In 1962, John was deemed mentally ill during a sanity hearing at the New Mexico District Court. He was committed to a state mental hospital in New Mexico. A condition of his release from the mental hospital in 1964, was that he move to Alaska and live with relatives. Instead, he headed for Washington state. He met Carol at a tavern in Portland shortly after he arrived on the west coast. He moved into her house two weeks before he murdered her children.

Detective Captain Eugene White of the Vancouver Police Department put out an all-points bulletin for the man who had the words, "born to lose" on his forearm along with the words "death before dishonor." Detective Captain White described the crime scene at Carol's house as the worst one he had seen in his twenty-one years on the job.

The autopsies revealed Bonnie and Fred suffered from blunt force trauma to the head and multiple stab wounds. The coroner reported Bonnie was stabbed in the heart and Fred was stabbed in the neck. Both victims had been hit numerous times with a hammer.

Both Bonnie and Fred were born and raised in Vancouver. Bonnie was in high school and Fred was attending middle school. Carol was separated from the children's father, who lived in Vancouver.

Two days after the dual homicides the U.S. Border Patrol located John in Blaine. He had attempted to cross the Canadian–United States border but did not have the funds to do so. He was unarmed at the time of his arrest and did not resist being taken into custody. He told the police he hitchhiked from Vancouver to Blaine, but Detective Captain White believed he stole a car near Carol's house. The car was abandoned in Chehalis with an empty gas tank. When John was arrested, he had a flashlight in his possession that belonged to the owner of the car.

John was transferred to the Clark County jail and charged with two counts of first-degree murder. He was placed under the tightest of security and held without bail.

Days later, a child found a knife near Carol's residence. The child's father turned the knife over to the police. Detectives located a hammer under Bonnie's bed they believed was the murder weapon. The hammer was sent to the F.B.I. in Washington, D.C. for analysis. The police collected clothing from Carol's laundry room they believed John wore when committing the murders. The clothing was turned over to a criminal pathologist.

Judge Virgil Scheiber appointed John LaLonde and Steven Memovich to represent John. Through his attorneys, John pled innocent and innocent by reason of insanity. Judge Scheiber agreed to have John examined by psychiatrist, Dr. Ivor Campbell. John's attorneys requested a change of venue citing the animosity in Clark County towards John. The prosecution contended, "There's going to be feeling wherever there are people who still have some compassion." The judge denied a motion for a change of venue, stating, "I sincerely feel he can get a fair trial here."

Dr. Campbell wrote in his report that John "is presently mentally ill and continues to have suicidal and paranoid ideations and is currently unable to assist counsel in his own defense." The doctor assessed extreme depression and apathy. Hearing this, Judge Eugene Cushing agreed to postpone the trial. Days later, John climbed on top of the shower wall, and unscrewed a lightbulb. He then broke the lightbulb and cut his forearms. A local doctor was called to attend to the cuts.

John's defense attorney, John LaLonda and Prosecuting Attorney DeWitt Jones traveled to New Mexico to view his criminal history. They learned more details about his court-ordered time in a mental hospital in 1962. In reviewing his records, they read where the court wrote:

The judge further found that defendant was unsafe to be at large and the defendant was committed to the state hospital...for the mentally insane under court order that he not be discharged without further order of that court and permission of the district attorney.

John's attorneys were granted two postponements while they reviewed his past criminal history. They asked that John be granted a sanity hearing and a third postponement saying they, "believe and have been advised by Dr. Ivor M. Campbell that to force the defendant to trial at this time would deprive the defendant of a fair and just trial for the reason that the defendant cannot properly assist in his own defense." They argued that John's extreme depression and apathy made it impossible for him to have enough interest to participate in his own defense. Superior Court Judge Guthrie Langsdorf countered that John did not show much interest in Dr. Campbell's testimony because, "He doesn't care for the gentleman, he doesn't want to assist and he showed it here in the courtroom while Dr. Campbell was testifying." Judge Langsdorf further stated:

> He also showed a very great deal of interest in Officer Winter's testimony. He certainly showed that he can show his interest if he so desires; and I'm sure that he can help the defendant's attorneys in the defense if he wants to.[1]

Prosecuting attorney Jones argued that John's inability to communicate with Dr. Campbell did not prove he was insane. He went onto say, "A mentally ill person under the civil act would not make him immune ... to prosecution under the provisions of criminal courts." Adding that, "If he just made up his mind that he wasn't going to talk about these unpleasant things" that did not make him insane.

The prosecution introduced letters written by John to his mother. Defense attorney Memovich immediately objected saying, "I'll object to any letters that may have been confiscated by the police and turned over to the prosecutor's office." He emphasized that the letters were seized illegally in violation of the Federal Communications Commission codes as well as John's constitutional rights. The judge allowed the letters to be read citing the fact that John signed a release allowing the prosecution to use the letters. The prosecution read letters and pointed out, "the writing, the paragraphing, the thought process showed a fairly high degree of coherence of thought."

After listening to both sides, Judge Langsdorf informed the attorneys, "I am satisfied that the entire matter can be determined in the trial next week. I am denying defendants both motions." He announced that the trial would begin the following Monday morning.

On Monday, May 17, 1965, sixty-seven people reported for jury duty in Judge Eugene Cushing's courtroom. The first dozen prospective jurors admitted they were opposed to the death penalty and were dismissed. Six individuals were dismissed after they admitted they had already decided the defendant was guilty. By the end of the day, seven women, five men, and two male alternates were impaneled as jurors.

The following morning after opening statements, Carol took the witness stand and told the jury the exact words John said when he met her at the door when she arrived home. She told of running to her daughter's bedroom downstairs. "First I called to her and she didn't answer me. Then I pulled her foot and she still didn't answer me. Then I noticed the covers were pulled over her head—and she never slept like that." Carol began sobbing as she told of realizing her daughter was dead. She said she ran to her neighbor's house and borrowed their telephone to call the police. She informed the jury that officers from the Vancouver Police Department arrived at her house and discovered both children deceased.

Carol fought back tears as she described meeting John. She said she had been separated from her husband for a year when she met John while working in a Portland tavern. She explained that she allowed John to move into her house but things were rocky from the start. John moved back to New Mexico after a couple of weeks at her house. Carol said she and the children wrote him a letter and after reading the letter he returned to live with them in Vancouver.

Carol told the jury about the evening her children were murdered. She said she asked Bonnie to drive her to a tavern in downtown Vancouver so she could meet with her estranged husband. Bonnie then went to visit a friend. She returned to the tavern later that evening but Carol was not ready to leave yet. Through tears, Carol said that was the last time she saw her daughter alive. Carol told the jury that a man at the tavern gave her a ride home. They talked outside for a few minutes before she headed to the door. It was there, she explained that John spoke those ominous words. He then said, "I guess you won't want me around here anymore." Even though at that moment she did not know the gravity of his words, Carol replied, "No, I don't. You cause too much trouble." At the time, she was referring to their recent arguments. She then stated, "he walked into the living room, grabbed his coat and ran out the door."

Carol was asked to identify clothing items that the police seized from her house that belonged to John. She also identified the claw hammer located under Bonnie's bed as one she kept in her kitchen. She was shown a knife that she identified as one from her kitchen. When asked if she ever married John in California, she vehemently denied it and stated she had never been to California. She emphasized at the time of the murders; she was still legally married to her estranged husband. She had since married another man, but again stated she was never married to John.

A deposition with John's mother was read to the jury. The deposition was taken at her house in New Mexico when John's defense attorneys visited her in an attempt to glean more information about their client. John's mother told the attorneys of the terrible headaches John suffered from most of his life. She recalled the last time she saw John was before he returned to Carol's house. She described his behavior as "ranting and raving." She added, "He didn't act normal or natural at all. He would pace from room to room and tear things." When the attorneys asked for clarification about John's behavior, his mother expanded by saying, "He would stomp around all over the house and curse ... It seemed like everything I said irritated him."

Alluding to a possible cause of mental illness, John's mother told of a time when John fell out of a tree and hit his head. She said he experienced paralysis for a few days, but did not receive medical care. She explained there was also a time during John's childhood when he fell off a bike and experienced temporary paralysis. She said he had also fallen off horses as a young boy.

John's mother said she witnessed John fall to the ground in her house shortly after being released from prison, before he moved to Washington. John's mother said he told her he and Carol were married in California. She said the reason John gave her for returning to New Mexico, was because, "they got drunk, he broke her arm and he thought the law was after him." A letter written by John to his mother was read to the jury: "I guess you know all about it from the newspapers. I can't remember anything about it, but if they say I did it, I guess I did."

Defense attorney LaLonde informed the jury after a tumultuous childhood, John enlisted in the military. He was given a general discharge for medical reasons. The defense pointed out that his military record showed, "discharged by virtue of his mental inability to matriculate or get along" in the military. After leaving the military, the defense explained, John got into trouble with the law and ended up in prison. Once released, he met a woman and brought her into the criminal justice system by having her help him in his criminal endeavors. They had a child together and later married. The marriage did not last and they went their separate ways.

Vancouver Police Detective Captain White explained his findings to the jury. He testified about the hammer located under Bonnie's bed saying, "it appeared to have blood on it and fibers or hair." The tests later confirmed, "human blood and human hair."

Tacoma criminal pathologist, Dr. Charles P. Larson, took the stand next and followed up with a more detailed explanation of the evidence from the crime scene. John's defense team objected to the weapons and clothing being admitted into evidence, stating there was no direct link to the murders. Judge Cushing overruled their objections. Dr. Larson admitted he was not able to determine the type of blood located on the knives or the hammer. However, he was able to determine the type of blood on clothing items the police located in a hamper in Carol's house. He explained to the panel of jurors that he found type AB blood on a bath towel, a pair of men's shoes, a pair of men's pants, and a man's shirt—Fred's blood type. He went on to say when John was captured, he was wearing a pair of pants that had blood stains from type A blood—Bonnie's type of blood.

Dr. Larson explained there were particles of human blood on the knife that the police found in a dresser drawer underneath some of John's clothing in his bedroom. He believed the blood was type A blood but cautioned he could not say for certain. When it came to the knife the child found in the neighborhood, he said there was no human blood on it. Additionally, it was not possible to lift fingerprints from any of the weapons.

Judge Cushing overruled defense attorney Memovich's objections to Dr. Larson showing color slides of the victim's wounds. Defense attorney Memovich argued the slides would "inflame and prejudice" the jury. The prosecution admitted the "pictures were not pretty." The jury viewed the slides on a projector in the courtroom. Dr. Larson was able to point out the four circular, "hammer-type" wounds on both children. He added there were blood stains above Bonnie's bed saying, "it was my opinion these spots were deposited by swinging of the hand or some instrument that had blood on it." John never looked at any of the slides.

Dr. Larson told the jury Fred was struck four times in the head with what he believed was a hammer. He further explained that Fred was initially standing up, but then fell onto his bed. John then allegedly slashed Fred's throat clear to his spine. The doctor told the jury that Fred drowned in his own blood, which was the cause of death. Bonnie's death, he explained, was similar in nature. She, too, was struck four times in the head with a hammer before being stabbed in the heart. The wound was approximately 6 inches deep, and "would have produced death within a matter of a few seconds."

During cross-examination, defense attorney Memovich asked Dr. Larson if the knife wounds or the hammer blows to the skull would "require a strong person?" Dr. Larson replied the attacker would not necessarily need strength. Dr. Larson admitted the blood stains on the knife and clothing could have been there for a period of time. Defense attorney Memovich honed in on the possibility by asking, "It's possible that the blood on the clothing had been on there for a number of years?" Dr. Larson answered, "that's possible, yes." Before defense attorney Memovich finished his cross-examination, he reminded the jurors the house was "left unguarded for some undetermined amount of time and the doors were left wide open," prior to the police finding the evidence.

U.S. Border Patrol Officer Dale Chorpenning told the jurors about stopping John just blocks from the Canadian–United States border. He said when he asked John for identification, John produced his driver's license from New Mexico. Officer Chorpenning told the jury when he looked at the driver's license, he remembered a police bulletin the Vancouver Police Department sent out. He placed John in the front seat of his patrol car while he notified the Whatcom County Sheriff's Department. Prosecutor Jones asked about John's demeanor, Officer Chorpenning stated, "He was coherent and civil and answered all my questions in a prompt manner."

Next on the witness stand was Whatcom County Deputy Dale Kruse. He told the jury he took custody of John from Officer Chorpenning and transported John to the county jail. Once there, he and Undersheriff Gus Johnson questioned him for approximately ten minutes. Deputy Kruse recalled John responded in a "normal" manner. When Undersheriff Johnson took the witness stand, he informed the jurists John spoke "like any other person" and gave "very clear and concise" answers.

Clark County Sheriff Clarence McKay testified about John's suicide attempt while at the county jail. The jury also learned about a time that John barricaded himself in his jail cell by breaking off a piece of metal from his bed and inserting it through the metal bars. Sheriff McKay also told the jury John had gone "on at least a couple" of hunger strikes when food was readily available to him.

Dr. Campbell testified that John admitted to him he took three types of illegal drugs the night of the murders. The drugs included a cough syrup containing a narcotic, some barbiturates, and a peyote drug. It was Dr. Campbell's testimony that the drugs produced "an acute brain syndrome." The jury listened as Dr. Campbell testified that John admitted to him that he murdered the teenagers.

The panel of jurists heard a deposition given by John's former Parole Officer, Michael Hanrahan. The deposition was taken when the defense and prosecution visited New Mexico. The jury learned that John was arrested in New Mexico in 1959 for grand larceny and contributing to the delinquency of a minor. He was sent to prison and paroled in 1961. Soon after being released from prison, John married and had a daughter, but the marriage did not last.

When defense attorney LaLonda and Prosecutor Jones travelled to New Mexico to learn more about John's criminal history, they spoke to psychiatrist Dr. Alan Jacobson. During a deposition, Dr. Jacobson told them John was convicted of kidnapping his estranged wife in 1962 and sent to a prison in New Mexico. After John made two suicide attempts while incarcerated, he was transferred to the state mental hospital, where he was examined by Dr. Jacobson. When asked about the crime that put him in prison, Dr. Jacobson stated in his deposition that John told him, "If I had it to do over again, I would kill my wife."

In the deposition, the psychiatrist stated it was his opinion that John would not benefit from rehabilitation in prison, and should remain in the state mental hospital. He believed John had "a schizoid type of personality." The doctor emphasized John was "very dangerous to himself, primarily," but he did add that he could also be a danger to society.

Parole Officer Hanrahan went onto explain in his deposition that the following year John stole two guns from his sister's house and went on a crime spree. John forced his estranged wife to accompany him. John robbed a gas station, carjacked a vehicle, and forced the driver to get into the trunk. He then drove the car for a period of time before agreeing to release his estranged wife at her urging and releasing the car's owner from the trunk. John went to his mother's house and hid in the attic where he remained during a five-hour standoff with the police. Parole Officer Hanrahan was present during the standoff and said in his deposition that at one point John shot at one of his brothers who tried to enter the house. The bullet missed the brother and narrowly missed Parole Officer Hanrahan. In his deposition, Parole Officer Hanrahan said that John was arrested at the end of the standoff and lodged at the Bernalillo County jail.

The jailer, Anthony Rey, from the Bernalillo County jail also provided a deposition. He described John's suicide attempts that ended with him being sent to the state mental hospital. The first attempt, he said, was when John swallowed several razor blades. The next attempt was after John's mother visited him and berated him for the publicity from his crime spree. He proceeded to climb up the jail bars and tied a blanket to the skylight. He attempted to hang himself but was cut down by jail staff.

In his closing remarks, Prosecutor Jones told the panel of jurists that John "bludgeoned" the brother and sister with a hammer before "plunging a knife into them with an almost surgical skill." He stated that John deliberately killed the children with cold premeditation, and while completely sane. He informed the jury, "Ironically, on the night when these children met their deaths, they had spoken out about this situation." He went onto say, "Mr. Hawkins is a defiant person. He is antisocial. He had indicated defiance ... at practically all stages of his life."[2]

Referring to the method of how Fred and Bonnie were murdered, the prosecution pointed out how precise his movements were, in contrast to an insane person. "This design of death ... was carried out with such a capability and a cunning and a knowledge that even if we felt that there was a question that Mr. Hawkins might have lost his head, as it were, we have the case of Bonnie."[3]

"After he had done Fred Walch in, he covered him up ... because John Hawkins knew that he wanted to kill Bonnie Walch and he didn't want her to see her brother's body." Referring to Bonnie's murder, he held up the hammer and showed it to the jury. "This was used for deliberate action. Did he hit her about the arms and body? He hit her about the head. He uses the hammer to anesthetize Bonnie. They were brutal blows; they were blows that a person of bestial nature would use..." Prosecutor Jones added, "Not having gotten her life with the hammer, then he uses the knife. This was used with an almost surgical skill."[4]

Before Prosecutor Jones rested, he pointed out that John took the time to change his clothes and to wait for Carol to return home; which he believed pointed to a sane person. He also reminded them of the words John said to Carol when she returned home.

The case was turned over to the jury. After twenty-one hours of deliberations, they found John guilty of first-degree murder for Bonnie. The jury found John innocent by reason of insanity for Fred. John's attorneys immediately moved for a new trial.

When questioned by reporters about the verdict, one juror explained they did not realize the implications of their verdict. Finding John guilty of first-degree murder meant that he would hang for the crime he committed. The juror told the media in part:

> In arriving at our verdict, I did not intend, and I am sure that most of the jurors did not intend that Mr. Hawkins would be sentenced to his death. It [was] my understanding that since we had found Mr. Hawkins not guilty by reason of insanity in the first charge, that Mr. Hawkins would have to be placed in an institution on the basis of this charge, and that he could not be sentenced on the second charge because the first charge would take precedence over the second charge.[5]

A new trial was denied and an execution date was set. The defense team filed an appeal based on their belief John should have had a sanity hearing as well as a change of venue. The appeal dragged on for two years before being denied by the State Supreme Court. John was ordered to report to the Clark County Superior Court on July 28, 1967, to receive a new date for his execution. He had been serving time on death row at the state penitentiary in Walla Walla.

On the morning of July 28, 1967, prison officials began the process of transporting John to the Clark County Superior Court. John was patted down for any weapons by three prison employees and run through an electric eye to make sure he did not have any weapons on him. He was placed in the back seat of a patrol car wearing handcuffs and leg irons that were attached to a chain that wrapped around his waist. Clark County Sheriff Deputy Stanley Jagelski and Clark County Sheriff Sergeant Llyod Smith were in the front seat which was separated by plexiglass from the back seat. As they traveled towards the courthouse, John spoke freely about the fishing he had done in the area years before and how he enjoyed painting.

It was about noon when the car entered a tunnel on Interstate 80N near the Bonneville Dam. Suddenly, John lunged at the plexiglass, reached his arm around the front seat, and grabbed Deputy Jagelski's .38-caliber revolver out of its holster. The deputy grabbed for his gun, but it was too late: John already had the weapon. At gunpoint, John demanded Sergeant Smith's weapon. Sergeant Smith was driving the car but he managed to reach down and pull it part way out of the holster. From there, John reached around and grabbed the gun. John then demanded Sergeant Smith pull off the highway onto a nearby road.

"These ball point pens are dangerous," said John as he showed the lawmen how he had freed himself of the handcuffs and leg irons. John had smuggled a makeshift key that he made from a component of a ball point pen and used it to free himself. He ordered both men out of the car at gun point and proceeded to chain them to a tree using the handcuffs, chain and leg irons. John got into the patrol car and took off at a high rate of speed, narrowly missing a bread truck traveling down the road.

The hostages managed to reach down and pick up a rock and hit the lock repeatedly until it sprang open. They ran a distance until they saw a man fishing nearby. The citizen gave them a ride to the nearest gas station where they were able to use a telephone. Sergeant Smith called the Multnomah County Sheriff's Office in Oregon and requested they begin a manhunt in their jurisdiction where John was last seen. He then phoned Sheriff McKay to let him know the prisoner was behind the wheel of their patrol car.

Sergeant Smith later told Neil Modie of *The Columbian*:

> He didn't threaten to kill us. But he would have without hesitation, I know. He was fairly cool. He watched us with those damned black eyes that looked just like a weasel, and I died about three times ... He stood there and stared at us. He pointed that gun at our bellies, and I just knew he was going to shoot. He said he wouldn't be taken alive, and he'd shoot anyone who tried.[6]

A few hours later, the Clark County Sheriff's patrol car was located hidden in thick brush near Dodson, Oregon. Deputy Jagelski's gun was left behind, but the ammunition was missing. The Oregon State Police and Washington State Patrol were joined by city and county law enforcement from both states in their search for the prison escapee. Bloodhounds were brought in to join the search which covered trails nearly inaccessible due to the terrain around the Columbia River Gorge. There were no reports of stolen vehicles or carjackings in the area, so law enforcement presumed John was on foot in the area. They knew he was well-versed at living off the land for periods of time in New Mexico and feared he could do the same for an extended period of time in Oregon or Washington. Roadblocks were set up in Hood River, Cascade Locks, and Troutdale, Oregon. Police were stationed at all bridges in the immediate area. The Vancouver Police Department placed Carol in protective custody, fearing John would return for her.

There was a brief moment of excitement when the police were notified of citizens hearing gunfire a few miles from Multnomah Falls. Numerous law enforcement officers responded to the area to find two boys target shooting. The boys were told to leave the area for their own safety.

Two days later, John was reported to have broken into a house in Dodson, startling the residents just after midnight. Later that morning, a rowboat was stolen from Dodson and recovered near Skamania.

North Bonneville Chief of Police Lewis Christensen and Skamania County Sheriff's Deputy Rodney Bevans spotted John while searching an abandoned cabin in the woods off Highway 830. They did not find John in the cabin, but when they looked through a window, they spotted his leg protruding from a tree. John fired one shot towards Chief Christensen, narrowly missing him. As he turned to fire at Deputy Bevans, Chief Christensen fired back, striking John in the back with shotgun pellets. John gave up and law enforcement moved in and captured their man, thus ending a four-day manhunt.

John appeared in court and was given a new execution date of September 17, 1967, approximately six weeks from his court appearance. The American Civil Liberties Union filed an application for a stay of execution. Washington State Governor Dan Evans granted a reprieve until all legal remedies were exhausted. The State Supreme Court denied the stay. The U.S. Supreme Court refused to review the petition filed by John's legal team.

While he was awaiting execution, the U.S. Supreme Court ruled that prospective jurors who were opposed to the death penalty could no longer be automatically excused from serving on a jury. Based on the new ruling, the Washington State Supreme Court granted a stay of execution for John long enough for the American Civil Liberties Union to present its case.

The State Supreme Court overturned John's death sentence. Six years after he was supposed to hang for the murder of Bonnie, Judge Robert McMullen sentenced John to life in prison as criminally insane. John married while serving time at the Washington State Hospital.

Six years later, he requested an unconditional release from the Washington State Hospital. A trial was held where many hospital staff testified on John's behalf. A therapy supervisor told the court, "At no time had he done anything that would indicate he was psychotic." A hospital ward testified, "John and I became sorta friends." He spoke of taking John out of the hospital an estimated fifty times, occasionally taking him to his house and to go fishing. The ward said he was John's best man when he married at the hospital. Another therapist told the court he believed John's marriage had taken away John's sociopath, antisocial personality. His bid for freedom was turned down. A few years later, John was released from the Washington State Hospital.

4
JUDGE LAWLESS

"We do not have a suspect at this time. We're attempting to run down any and all leads." Those words were spoken by Franklin County Sheriff Richard Boyles in describing the murder of Superior Court Judge James L. Lawless who was killed by what the sheriff believed was a "well-made pipe bomb" on June 3, 1974, in Pasco.

The pipe bomb was described as a 4-inch pipe filled with an explosive material. It was housed in a wooden box wrapped in white paper. The entire package was wrapped in brown paper. Judge Lawless was killed instantly when he opened the package in his chambers. Twenty inspectors from the United States Postal Service, the F.B.I., and the U.S. Treasury Department of Alcohol, Tobacco, and Firearms Bureau arrived at the Franklin County courthouse to investigate.

Judge Lawless had served on the bench for seventeen years. He served in both Pasco and Prosser and was well respected in both towns. Judge Lawless and his wife, Beth, had five children. When he was first appointed judge at the age of thirty-three, he was one of the youngest judges to ever hold the position in Washington state. Ten years later, Judge Lawless was the youngest judge in the state to hear a State Supreme Court case when he was appointed justice *pro tem*.

The investigators working the pipe bombing case were left with more questions than answers. Although Judge Lawless had not been involved with any recent controversial case, the explosion came on the heels of four suspicious fires in April 1974. A Prosser police officer was the victim of an arson at his house. Hours later, a fire broke out at another local house. Soon after a fire broke out at the Prosser High School and at the Prosser United Presbyterian Church. Additionally, a Benton County Sheriff's car had been bombed.

At the conclusion of the investigation into the four arson fires, the investigators arrested Ricky Anthony Young (A.K.A. Anthony Mario Ragusin), age twenty-three. Although there had been four arson fires committed in a short period of time, the investigators were only able to determine that Ricky was involved with two of the fires. Ricky was renting the house where one of the arson fires took place. Ricky was charged with two counts of arson and a trial date was set with Judge Lawless presiding over the trial.

This was not the first time Ricky appeared before Judge Lawless. In 1971, Judge Lawless sentenced Ricky to a term of fifteen years in prison for a burglary at Phil's Drug Store. Judge Lawless stipulated he would suspend the sentence as long as Ricky served one year in the Benton County jail on the burglary charge.

In another case that Judge Lawless oversaw, Ricky was accused of abducting a sixteen-year-old girl. Judge Lawless ordered Ricky to not have any contact with the sixteen-year-old girl. Ricky was never formally charged with the abduction, and the sixteen-year-old girl later became his wife. Ricky filed an affidavit of prejudice against Judge Lawless. For that reason, Judge Lawless recused himself from Ricky's upcoming arson trial.

The United States Post Office offered a $10,000 reward for information leading to the conviction of the person(s) responsible for the murder of Judge Lawless. A local reward in the amount of $2,193 was also offered. The investigators went through every case Judge Lawless ever worked in his seventeen years on the bench. More than twenty people who had recently appeared before Judge Lawless were asked to take a polygraph test. All of those who took the polygraph test passed without any problems.

Two months after the pipe bombing, the investigators determined Ricky was responsible for sending the pipe bomb. Ricky was charged with first-degree murder in Franklin County. He was also charged with the federal offense of manufacturing and delivering of a nonmailable matter with intent to kill or injure. Ricky pled innocent to all charges.

Ricky went on trial for two counts of arson at the Superior Court in Tacoma. One case involved a home where Ricky and his wife lived. The other case was for the arson at the Prosser United Presbyterian Church. A police officer testified that he saw Ricky receiving treatment for burns on his face and torso at a hospital in Yakima. He added that the defendant's arm was heavily bandaged.

Ricky's wife told the court, the only time he was burned was when he attempted to burn several boxes of love letters that she had written to him over a period of time. A friend of Ricky's testified Ricky admitted to him that he was responsible for the arson fires and asked him to provide an alibi. Ricky took the witness stand and denied his involvement in either of the arson fires.

The jury was sequestered at a local motel every night during the six-day trial. The jury deliberated five hours before finding Ricky guilty on two counts of arson. He received a sentence of five to twenty years in prison for the crimes.

Six months after the bomb killed Judge Lawless, the trial got underway in Spokane County Superior Court with Judge William H. Williams presiding. The jury was made up of eight men and four women. Franklin County Prosecuting Attorney Clarence Rabideau and Spokane County Prosecuting Attorney Norris Barnhill represented the state of Washington. Ricky's defense attorney, Sidney Wurzburg, told the media, "It will certainly be an interesting trial."

Federal Investigator Jim Reeves took the witness stand and told the panel of jurists he responded to the crime scene in Judge Lawless' chambers. He said he used tweezers and picked up pieces of evidence left from the explosion. He explained once back at his laboratory, he studied all of the evidence. He discovered several tiny fragments of paper that he put back together like a jigsaw puzzle. From his expertise, he knew those minuscule pieces had come from the package that held the pipe bomb.

James Upton, a chemist with the United States Postal Service's crime lab in Washington, D.C., testified he examined a piece of tape that was on the back of a paper shred from the wrapping. That shred of paper held two fingerprints. He was able to discern that one fingerprint belonged to Ricky. The second fingerprint he located was on a shred of paper underneath a grain of the powder used in the pipe bomb. He told the jury he was not able to identify the second fingerprint.

To counter the chemist's identification of Ricky's fingerprint, the defense put a professor from Washington State University on the stand. He testified the fingerprint in question could not be identified. He said he found at least nine discrepancies that could not be attributed to Ricky.

The jury learned about Ricky's past contacts with Judge Lawless. Prosecutor Rabideau informed the jury:

> The state's theory is that this device was delivered to the judge through efforts of the defendant because he was aware of two things—he stood a good chance of going to a corrections center and of losing contact with his wife. He wanted to eliminate the person who had threatened to take him away from the community and who might again take him away from the woman who was now his wife.[1]

Three postal clerks testified about handling the package. They said the package was addressed to Justice James J. Lawless and had the word "personal" on it. The package was picked up at the post office by a chief deputy clerk who transported it to the courthouse. A court reporter took the package to Judge Lawless' chambers. She told the jury:

> He [Lawless] was sitting at his desk reading. I handed him the package and said something like, "Judge, I've brought you a package from Prosser." I started back down the hall, and was in my office for maybe two minutes when I heard this roar. It was loud, like an explosion. I ran back, and met Judge Yencopal. He had a shocked look on his face and was gesturing towards Judge Lawless' office. We walked down the hall together. He looked into the judge's door first. Then he told me not to look.[2]

Despite the defense's objections, the prosecution was allowed to have the court transcripts from Ricky's contacts with Judge Lawless read to the jury. The jury also heard from Dr. Ivan LeCompte, a pathologist who conducted the autopsy on Judge Lawless. Dr. LeCompte explained to the jury that the judge died from a piece of metal that pierced his heart.

In his closing remarks, Prosecuting Attorney Rabideau told the jury Ricky committed this "heinous crime" because "he knew the handwriting was on the wall" and that Judge Lawless would probably send him to prison based on a recent report from his probation officer. He said a probation revocation hearing was scheduled in front of Judge Lawless. Summing up he told the panel of jurists, "When you couple that motive with the fingerprint in the bomb and his knowledge of the bomb, the evidence is overwhelming that he is guilty."

Defense attorney countered by saying, "This crime was an assassination, worse than a murder. It did great violence to our system. But now I implore you to not do the system a greater violence by convicting an innocent man." He stated the fingerprint could have been placed on the paper at a later date.

> You do not have to decide whether Rick has been in trouble before, if he is a bad guy or if he knew about what was going on with the bomb. You have to decide if he killed Judge Lawless. The state, at best, has shown possibilities, but it hasn't proven anything.

The panel of jurors agreed and were unable to reach a verdict. Judge Williams declared a mistrial. A date was selected for a new trial.

While awaiting his next trial, Ricky made a bid for freedom at the Yakima County jail. Ricky and two other inmates attempted to overpower Yakima County jail deputy Fred Smith. They tried to tie him up but were unsuccessful, and he managed to break free of the inmates. As it turned out, even if they had been successful, a second door was locked and would have prevented as escape. Ricky was charged with second-degree assault but the charges were later dismissed.

Six months after the first trial, a second trial got underway for the murder of Judge Lawless. Spokane County Superior Court Judge John Lally presided. The new jury heard the evidence from the first trial but they also heard from Ricky's cellmate. The cellmate informed the jury that Ricky confessed to him and gave details about building the bomb. The jury heard from Ricky's wife, mother, and stepfather, all of whom provided an alibi for the day the package was mailed. Ricky's wife named a friend of theirs as the prime suspect.

This time the jury agreed with the prosecution and found Ricky guilty of first-degree murder. Ricky's defense lawyer, Sidney Wurzburg was granted a delay in sentencing so he could conduct an investigation into how the jury came to their conclusion. He was convinced someone had tampered with the jury.

Defense attorney Wurzburg was only able to contact nine members of the jury. Those he spoke to denied any jury tampering and stated they believed Ricky was guilty because his fingerprint was on the paper surrounding the pipe bomb. They also believed Ricky did not like Judge Lawless. Learning this, defense attorney Wurzburg told the court that his client's conviction was "based entirely on circumstantial evidence. Those fingerprints are capable of many interpretations and guilty is not necessarily one of them." He asked Judge Lally to order each juror to testify as to how they came to their decision, but Judge Lally denied the request.

While awaiting sentencing on the murder charge, Ricky went on trial for bombing the Benton County patrol car. The trial lasted one day with two of Ricky's former friends testifying. One friend told the jury that Ricky asked him on three different occasions to accompany him when he placed the bomb in the car. He stated Ricky's wife was present, as was the other friend, when the request was made.

Ricky's other friend recalled being asked to help bomb the car, but he testified "I didn't take him seriously." Ricky's wife attended the trial, but did not testify. Before the jury began deliberations, Ricky's defense attorney reminded the jury that just because Ricky talked about bombing the car did not mean he did it. The jury felt otherwise and returned a verdict of guilty. Ricky was sentenced to five years in federal prison for bombing the patrol car. The sentence was to start after his other arson sentence was completed.

The defense for the murder trial requested a new trial. Judge Lally denied the defense's request. During the sentencing hearing, Judge Lally told Ricky, he had, "never seen a man charged with homicide who was more vigorously and adequately defended than your counsel has done in this case." Ricky replied, "I am innocent and I am sure the truth will come out." Judge Lally sentenced Ricky to life imprisonment, the maximum sentence available. In his documentation to the parole board, Judge Lally stressed the word "life."

Prosecutor Rabideau wrote in his recommendation to the parole board:

> Had the death penalty been available at the time this case was tried, the undersigned would have asked for a death verdict.... Jim Lawless was a career jurist; it is difficult to encourage people with his intelligence, insight and compassion to become jurists at any time. He was at the prime of his career when snuffed out by the wantonness of the defendant.

In summing up his recommendation to the parole board, Prosecutor Rabideau wrote that Ricky, "should ROT in prison so that others like him will hopefully be deterred from terrorizing the judiciary, one of the bastions of freedom in this country. I apologize to no one for this recommendation."[3]

A fellow inmate of Ricky's filed a lawsuit on his behalf. The $750,000 lawsuit alleged Ricky was being falsely imprisoned. After one clerk attempted to decipher it, she said, "Nearly every other word in the lawsuit is misspelled and it's impossible to read, let alone understand."

The Washington State Supreme Court upheld the conviction on both the arson and murder cases. They later refused to reconsider their decision. The U.S. Supreme Court declined to review Ricky's murder case.

Ricky was first sent to McNeil Island prison. He was transferred ten times over a short period of time, but wherever he went, problems ensued. After four years his incident report totaled forty-four pages. While serving time at the Walla Walla prison, a pipe bomb exploded, killing one guard and injuring two others in 1978. An eighteen-day lockdown followed. Ricky used red paint to write derogatory remarks about the guards who were injured and the one who died. He spent time in federal prisons in Oregon, Tennessee, and Arizona in the first decade of his incarceration. Ricky filed a petition with the Washington State of Appeals citing the transfers were an undue hardship on his wife. Assistant Attorney General David Minikel stated Ricky and others were transferred because "we had lost control of the prison and he had to be removed so we could regain control."

Ricky became the center of a decision as to whether or not a prisoner was entitled to a hearing before being placed in segregation. The Department of Social and Health Services filed a petition stating it was not necessary. In their report, they wrote in part that Ricky was a "negative leadership influence on the prison and a threat to the security of the institution." Their report indicated Ricky may have been responsible for the bomb that killed the prison guard. The Washington State Supreme Court ruled Ricky was entitled to a hearing prior to being placed in segregation and before being transferred.

In 2016, Ricky's new attorneys requested that the evidence from the pipe bomb be tested for D.N.A. Their request was denied. As of 2023, Ricky remains a prisoner within the Washington Department of Corrections.

5
WILLIAM O. FISHER

In July 1948, a family was enjoying a picnic in Skamania County when their otherwise peaceful day was shattered when they discovered a man's body in some bushes. Sheriff deputies from Skamania County responded to the crime scene.

The deceased man was identified as William O. Fisher, age fifty-three. The detectives were able to determine he was from Portland, Oregon, and worked as a union business agent for the Masters and Mates Union based in Portland. William had been shot in the chest twice and badly beaten.

On the day after the discovery of the body, Skamania County Deputies Dale Hess and Ted Hanson stopped a car for running a stop sign. The driver did not have a driver's license. Neither of the two men—Harold Raymond Coe, age seventeen, or Lewis Donald Lillard, age twenty—were able to answer the questions posed to them. The police searched the car and located a .22-caliber weapon and a check made out to William in the amount of $1,500.

The two men were transported to the Clark County jail for further questioning. Lewis confessed to the murder saying he shot William and pushed him down an embankment. In his confession, he stated that robbery was the motive for the homicide. Lewis told the detectives William picked them up when they were hitchhiking. He recalled they drove for a period of time and then stopped at a tavern. When they were back in the car, Lewis hit William over the head with a .38-caliber pistol.

He said when William reached for his own weapon, Lewis shot him. Lewis told the detectives they dragged William out of the car and rolled the body down an embankment. He admitted to taking cash and $2,500 in bonds from William. He said they drove William's car to Portland and abandoned it near a golf course.

Lewis said they retrieved a vehicle that belonged to Harold's father. He said the following day they drove to Camas and went swimming. They were on their way to a friend's party in McLoughlin Heights when they were stopped by the police. Lewis admitted to the police, both he and Harold were AWOL from the U.S. Navy where they had been stationed in San Diego.

Harold told Skamania County Sheriff Amos Reid and Investigator Harold Quarnberg that William picked them up while they were hitchhiking. They drove for a while then went to a tavern near Cape Horn where they all consumed alcohol. As they were leaving, he got in the front passenger seat and Lewis got in the back. He recalled Lewis hitting William who turned towards the back seat while reaching for his gun. "That is when Lillard started firing. I got down on the floor boards." Harold recalled William crying, "Don't kill me, don't kill me!" Harold went onto say:

> He started to slump my way in the car and I got out of the car and I took two steps backwards and slipped down over the bank. When I got back up, Lillard had the man out of the car and he told me that I had better help him as I was in as deep as he was. We drug the body out of the car and down over the bank to where it was later found. Lillard opened the front of his trousers to see if he had a money belt.[1]

Harold said he found William's wallet on the ground and stole $24 from it. Harold said they got in William's car and began driving through Camas and Washougal. He recalled going to Portland and parking the car. He said they searched the entire car and placed any documents they found in William's hat. "We found the bonds, I believe, in the glove compartment; two $1,000 bonds and a $50 bond and a $25 bond. Lillard had his gun in his holster and the man's gun was in his pocket."

Harold explained they were unable to get the car started after they stopped in Portland. As they were pushing the car down the street, a police officer with the Portland Police Bureau stopped them. Harold said Lewis showed the officer the registration from the car and explained they were just pushing the car, not driving it. The police officer remarked, "everything was all right." Harold remembered, that as the police officer walked away, "Lillard said that the policeman didn't know how close he came to getting holes in him."

Harold recalled he and Lewis slept in William's car for a while and then went to a repair shop and picked up his father's car. They purchased a car battery for William's car and Lewis drove that car while Harold followed in his father's car. They drove towards the golf course off Union Avenue.

When William's car stalled, they abandoned it, but not before they checked it over for evidence. They located a spent shell. They wiped the car down for fingerprints and tossed William's hat and papers into the river.

After that, Harold explained, they drove his father's car back to Camas. They went on a picnic with Harold's family at Little White Salmon River. They climbed Beacon Rock before returning to the Coe's residence and going to bed. Harold said the next day the duo visited friends and swan in Lacamas Lake. They were heading to a party in McLoughlin Heights, Harold said, when they were stopped by the police.

When the police searched Harold's house, they located the murder weapon. Harold said he did not know what happened to the gun, but Lewis admitted he hid it in a fishing tackle box at the Coe's house. When shown the gun, Lewis admitted it was the weapon used to murder William.

Lewis and Harold were charged with first-degree murder, robbery, and grand larceny. Harold's attorney requested and was granted a separate trial from Lewis. Both men pled innocent.

Before Lewis's trial was to start, he pled guilty to second-degree murder. He was sentenced to life in prison. Harold's trial got underway on September 17, 1948. Harold wore his U.S. Navy uniform and appeared nervous as he sat next to his attorney. His parents were present, as was William's wife.

The jury heard from the law enforcement officers who discovered William's body and those who interviewed Harold and Lewis. Dr. Sneeden, a physician and surgeon and a professor of pathology at the University of Portland, testified about his findings when he conducted the autopsy on William. Skamania County Sheriff Reed testified about responding to the crime scene and his interview with Harold. Washington State Patrol officer Dick Reaksecker told of locating the stolen bonds inside the book *Heidi* at Harold's house. He told the jury Harold admitted he had placed the bonds in the book. He also testified about finding the stolen $24 at Harold's house.

Lewis took the witness stand and admitted to firing the gun, but said Harold was the one who beat William. Lewis testified that he and Harold decided to rob William while they were drinking at the tavern. Once they were on the road, he said, he hit William over the head. He admitted to firing his gun when he thought William was reaching for his own gun. He recalled William crying, "I'm hit!" Lewis admitted the two of them dragged William out of his car and went through his pockets before they pushed him down the embankment. He told the jury they stole $2,050 in bonds and $24 in cash.

Harold took the witness stand and placed the blame squarely on Lewis. He denied ever planning to rob the victim or hitting him. He told the court he got down on the floorboards when Lewis began firing his gun. He admitted to helping pull William out of the car because he feared Lewis would shoot him. Prosecutor DeWitt Jones asked why he did not leave Lewis and tell someone what happened? Harold replied that Lewis kept him close by the entire time. Harold said after the murder they went to a drive-in and drank some milk.

Harold said he tried to "ditch" Lewis when they were driving separate cars the morning after the murder. He told the jury he went off on a side road but found the road blocked. Soon after, he said, Lewis pulled up next to him and yelled, "What are you trying to do?" Harold admitted he assisted in wiping their fingerprints from William's car before abandoning it. He told the court about going on a picnic with his family, going swimming the next day, and visiting with friends.

The jury deliberated for five hours before finding Harold guilty of first-degree murder and robbery. The jury did not recommend the death penalty, meaning Harold would be sentenced to life in prison. The robbery conviction added another twenty years, but the sentences were to run concurrently.

Four years later, Harold was back in the news. On December 23, 1952, Harold was one of seven inmates who dug a 200-foot tunnel underneath the Walla Walla prison by removing an estimated 12 tons of dirt, one handful at a time for many months. The tunnel began at the ash pit near the prison powerhouse. The prison officials believed the dirt was mixed in with the ashes and carted off each day. The diameter of the tunnel was approximately fifteen inches and came out past a guard tower on the north wall. The seven inmates who escaped worked the overnight shift in the powerhouse and were not guarded during their shift. However, the prison officials believed the men would have only been able to dig for a short period of time each shift and would have only been able to mix a small amount of dirt in with the ash each shift. The investigators believed the seven escapees left during a change of guard at 7 a.m. and stole a car nearby.

As it turned out, Harold was back behind bars in time for Christmas. All law enforcement was notified to be on the lookout for a vehicle that had been stolen in Walla Walla the day of the escape. Officers Ralph Pope and Ray Judson, spotted the stolen car near the Oregon–Washington border. The driver of the car pulled into a gas station, without realizing a state patrol car was directly behind him. Harold and his fellow escapee, Merrill Case, serving time for burglary, were arrested and returned to the prison.

6
FRANK TODD

When Frank Todd heard a knock on his door late at night, he did not hesitate to open the door. The following morning his wife, Ethel, found him dead in their woodshed, just steps from their house, having been beaten to death.

Frank, age thirty-five, worked as a logger. He and Ethel had two young children. The family made their home in Hoquiam. On the night of August 31, 1907, Ethel went upstairs to go to bed, while Frank stayed downstairs reading a book in the front room of their house. Ethel woke about 5 a.m. and noticed Frank was not in bed. She assumed he had fallen asleep while reading and went to look for him. There was a light on in the front room, and the door was wide open. She found Frank lying in a pool of blood just outside their door, in their woodshed.

The police arrived and determined Frank had been hit over the head with a blunt object, possibly an ax. Ethel told the police she believed Frank had $100 in his pocket at the time he was assaulted. When the police checked Frank's pockets, they were empty. The police did locate a blood-soaked handkerchief and a pocketknife, both of which they presumed were dropped by the killer. The police sent for bloodhounds hoping they would lead to the murderer but they did not have any luck.

Coroner Girford and Dr. Hunter conducted an autopsy. They were able to determine Frank had been hit on the forehead with such great force that the fractured portion of his skull had been driven into his brain.

A service for Frank was held at the Todd's house. After the service, hundreds of loggers and fraternal orders walked from the house to the burial site to pay their respects.

The City Council of Hoquiam offered a $100 reward for the apprehension and conviction of the person(s) responsible. Ethel was appointed the executor of Frank's estate and the guardian of their children.

One week after the murder, a man by the name of Andrew Strong confessed to murdering Frank. He was arrested and lodged in jail. Andrew told the authorities two men forced him to murder Frank, but he was not willing to name anyone. In his confession, he said he was paid $200 for the murder.

The police were not convinced Andrew was responsible for the crime, mainly because he did not know enough details about the murder. They were more interested in Ralph Steele. Ralph and two of his friends had rented a room in the upstairs of the Todd home weeks before the murder took place. Three weeks into his jail stay, Andrew took his own life. He managed to take a piece of rope that was woven into his mattress and use that to hang himself from his cell bars.

Ralph, who also went by the name of Herbert Norman, worked at a logging camp near the East Hoquiam River. His job involved pumping water from the river to the logging camp. Frank was the foreman of a logging camp about a dozen miles down the road.

Frank's workers told the detectives that the morning Frank's body was discovered, Ralph came into their camp at daybreak completely disheveled. They noted his clothes were torn to bits and it appeared he had been crawling through heavy brush. When questioned as to why he was at their camp, he simply said he had been sleepwalking. This seemed implausible to those at the camp because they knew he would have had to cross sloughs, fallen trees, and thick brush to get to their camp. The workers told the police about a rumor they heard wherein Frank pointed a rifle at Ralph, but no one knew the details.

Soon after Frank was murdered, the following article ran in newspapers throughout Washington state:

> Ralph Steele who has been suspected of the murder of Frank Todd, has been cleared of all complicity in the affair. Steele has been persecuted for weeks, some going so far as to publicly state their belief in his guilt. He has been under police surveillance, though the police have thought him innocent. His connection with the case came about through his possession of a revolver, a hammer and a pair of shoes which were apparently stained with blood. He turned these over to the police, who submitted them to expert examination, as a result of which Steele's innocence is established.[1]

After the police publicly exonerated Ralph, they put him under surveillance. They watched as he attended Frank's funeral. They watched him while he was working and after work, but they had nothing to report. Marshal McKenney learned that Ethel may have had an intimate relationship with Ralph in the months leading up to her husband's murder.

Marshal McKenney requested that Ethel meet with Ralph on several occasions when he could be within earshot. The meetings took place, but did not generate any news for weeks. Finally, Ralph confessed to Ethel that he murdered her husband, all the while stating he did it because he was in love with her.

Marshal McKenney trailed Ralph to his home one day in November 1907, but Ralph discovered he was under surveillance. He walked in his front door and immediately walked out the back door and hid in some bushes. As Marshal McKenney walked past the bushes, Ralph fired one shot, narrowly missing him. Ralph returned to his house. Three police officers knocked on the door. Ralph opened the door but quickly shut it, once he realized who was on his doorstep. The officers forced their way in and took Ralph into custody.

Two months later, Marshall McKenney told reporters, "Steele is arrested for murder and we have enough evidence to hang him. The evidence is conclusive and there has been no mistake made." The police explained they made the decision to exonerate Ralph publicly in the newspaper in the hopes he would relax his guard and do or say something that would make it possible for them to arrest him.

Ralph's attorney, William Abel, believed someone assisted Ralph with the murder. He told the press:

> Frank Todd was chloroformed, dragged out to the woodshed, then foully murdered, and Steele did not do the deed alone. The crime was one of the most diabolical ever known in the history of this county and some very damaging evidence will be brought out in the near future. I spent two hours with Steele yesterday and listened to his confession with horror. It unnerved me, as I had never heard of such a rule. Sometime soon I will make a statement in Steel's behalf, but not now.[2]

The police did not believe Frank was chloroformed or dragged out to the woodshed. They believed Ralph struck Frank as he stepped outside of his house. However, there were records at Grays Harbor Drug Store proving Ethel did purchase chloroform. She explained to the druggist she needed the product for cleaning clothes. Ethel also purchased laudanum, saying it was for her husband. Dr. Watkins confirmed that he did prescribe the medicine for Frank.

Ralph was only behind bars a short while before committing suicide by hanging. The jail staff found letters written by Ralph to Ethel. One letter read in part:

Now I want to say here and now and for all time that I will never give you up and live. If ever the time comes that I make up my mind that I must give you up then life will be very short. I love you to madness, to insanity I suppose, but I can't help it. I love you just the same with all the heart and soul that is in me. I know that I have said and written some awful mean things to you, but the truth is that I love you so and want you so bad that when I get to worrying about you it drives me mad.[3]

A friend of Ralph's was arrested the day after his suicide after he threatened Marshal McKenney. He was overheard saying, "The next time someone takes a shot at you you won't be so lucky."

After Ralph committed suicide, the Hoquiam City Council questioned law enforcement if everything had been done to solve the murder. The police confirmed they had done everything to solve the homicide. When William was asked about his client, he informed them Ralph had confessed to him while in jail.

In his confession, Ralph allegedly told William that Ethel had made previous attempts on her husband's life by poisoning him with laudanum. Her motive, William explained, was so she could marry Ralph. William explained Ralph told him on the night of the murder, Ethel drugged Frank's beer with laudanum, but he only got sick. She then gave him some whiskey which was also spiked with laudanum. After he passed out, Ralph said Ethel chloroformed him and together they dragged his body out to the woodshed. It was Ralph's statement that Ethel struck the first blow, and he completed the murder.

Once the public learned of William's statement to the city council, they wanted more details. William told reporters that Ethel offered to pay Ralph's legal fees if he would defend Ralph. William added that Ethel told him she was afraid of Ralph. William admitted at first, he turned the offer down, but then decided to accept the money. According to William, after Ralph took his own life, Ethel told him:

It was not necessary for Steele to murder my husband in order to get me. I loved him and he could have had me without that. We were planning to elope, though, after Mr. Todd was killed, but I made up my mind that Steele was only after my money, so I confessed.[4]

When questioned about the statement, Ethel told reporters:

Yes, I have seen the Abel story in regard to what Steele said and am not surprised as I expected something would be said of this nature. I have nothing to say, as there is nothing to say and I know the only thing I can do is to stand and take what is said about me.[5]

Ethel gave a written statement to Marshal McKenney. Many of the details in the written statement differed from what Ethel had originally told the police. In her statement she admitted she knew Frank had been murdered before daylight. In this version she said she heard a noise outside "as if wood was falling." She wrote about going outside and seeing Frank on the ground and someone standing over him. Ethel wrote in part:

> I fainted and knew nothing for some time. When I came to, I was in bed and Steele was sitting beside me with a revolver in his hand and when I cried, he told me it was no use as the deed was done and he did it for me because he wanted me and there was no other way, only if I was going to break down he would finish the job and kill me and himself. He stayed and talked to me till 3 o'clock and then I got up after he had gone to see if Frank was really dead. I stayed in the shed with him a little while and then went back in the house … He told me that nobody would suspect him, but if they did they would suspect me too and that they would hang both of us.[6]

Ethel was never charged with her husband's murder. Ethel and her children left Hoquiam and purchased a property in Mantesano for $2,500.

7
FANNY RICE

Detective Captain Al Farrar described the murder as "about the most rugged case I have ever seen." He was describing the murder scene in October 1950 wherein Fanny Rice, age eighty-four, was raped and murdered in the utility room of her house in Tacoma.

Fanny's husband died three years before and she lived alone. She devoted her life to helping the less fortunate. Fanny and three of her neighbors had devised a system so they each could check on one another. One part of the system was Fanny raised her blinds to a certain level each day to let her neighbors know she was okay. When her neighbors noticed the blinds had not been raised, they retrieved a hidden key from the woodshed and entered Fanny's house. They found Fanny in her blood-soaked laundry room.

The police admitted they had little to go on. There was no weapon found at the crime scene and no witnesses. They believed the murderer had wiped his bloody hands on Fanny's blouse that he had ripped off her body.

Coroner Paul Mellinger reported Fanny's skull had been crushed to "small pieces, every rib broken and her body covered with bruises." He believed the murder weapon could have been a large piece of wood. The coroner estimated she had been hit fifteen to twenty times with the murder weapon.

Two weeks later, the police identified Carl Johan Pederson, age thirty, as a suspect. Carl had been a neighbor of Fanny's and had not been seen since Fanny was murdered. Carl's fingerprints were located at the crime scene. Detectives located a bloody fingerprint under a kitchen table as well as a bloody palm print on a cigar wrapper at the crime scene. Witnesses recalled seeing him near Fanny's house the afternoon she was murdered.

Carl was born in Montana, but the family moved to Norway when he was three years old. During World War II, Carl was arrested by the Germans for being a member of an underground Norwegian group. He was placed in a Nazi concentration camp until freed at the end of the war. By the time he returned to America in 1950 to visit relatives in King County, he had relinquished his American citizenship. Shortly before the murder, Carl had been ordered to leave the United States after officials learned he had taken a job at a shipyard which was a violation of his tourist visa. When the police in Tacoma learned Carl was from Norway, they requested international assistance in locating him.

When the ship liner the *Stockholm* pulled into Goteborg, Sweden, the Swedish police arrested Carl and held him for the United States authorities. Carl had boarded the ship in New York and sailed to Sweden. The police in Sweden searched his luggage but did not find anything of interest. They questioned him about the murder, but he was unable to explain his whereabouts the night Fanny was murdered.

The state department began the extradition process. The United States and Sweden had an agreement to extradite prisoners within sixty days of their capture. The arrest warrant for first-degree murder was sent by telegram to Sweden.

Carl fought extradition to America and the sixty days came and went. Sweden agreed to return Carl even though the extradition agreement had expired. An entire year passed and the prisoner remained in Sweden.

Carl's home country of Norway learned about the case from all of the publicity carried in newspapers around the globe. Norway and the United States did not have an extradition agreement when Carl was arrested. Officials in the United States feared Sweden would turn Carl over to the Norwegian government and they would never be able to prosecute him.

Sweden's Supreme Court ruled Carl should be returned to the United States to face a charge of first-degree murder citing that there was no obstacle in the way of returning him. After nearly two years of fighting to bring the prisoner back to America, Pierce County Prosecutor John O'Connell explained to the Associated Press:

We have done everything in our power to get him. We are drafting another letter now.... Sweden's courts have said now there is no legal reason for not returning him. Now the authorities presumably are checking whether there is any executive government reason. The only reason he has not been returned for trial is that Sweden has not granted clearance.[1]

Days before the two-year anniversary of Carl's arrest, Detective Carl Petersen with the Tacoma Police Department arrived in Sweden to retrieve his prisoner. Once back on American soil, Carl was booked into the Tacoma city jail. He appeared at a hearing in Pierce County and was formally charged with first-degree murder. The Norwegian government retained attorney, Tracy Griffin, of Seattle. He was granted additional time to review the case before Carl entered a plea. Prosecutor O'Connell told reporters, "I am anxious to try Pedersen. I am certain we have enough evidence against him to submit the case to a jury."

While Carl's attorney was reviewing the case, Axel Heiberg arrived from Norway to assist. He was an attorney and an attaché of the Norwegian Supreme Court. The Norwegian government covered the costs of Carl's defense team. Prosecutor O'Connell explained having the Norwegian official in Pierce County was the reason he placed Carl in the city jail, rather than the county jail. "If that judge ever got a look at our county jail, our foreign relations with Norway would hit a new low."

By the time the courtroom doors opened, it had been two-and-a-half years since Fanny had been murdered. A translator was on hand to translate for Carl, who informed the court he was unable to understand very much English. Sverre Gjellum, Norwegian vice counsel from San Francisco, and Christen Stang, Norwegian consul from Seattle, were in the courtroom representing Norway. Gaspar Brockman, a journalist from Oslo, Norway, flew to Pierce County to cover the trial for his readers at home. He was joined by Theo Findahl, a foreign correspondent based in New York. United Nations Delegate Gunderson was also in the courtroom to assist with Carl's defense.

Tacoma Police Chief Identification Officer Captain R. K. Henderson testified he found Fanny's purse near a dresser in her house. He went on to say the lining of the black purse was torn. He added that the bottom drawers in her dresser were wide open. The investigation, he explained, showed Fanny had cashed her pension check the afternoon she was murdered.

Captain Henderson described finding a cigar and a cigar wrapper, both of which he personally took to the F.B.I. Laboratory in Washington, D.C. Captain Henderson requested that a leaf from Fanny's table be admitted into evidence. He explained to the judge, the leaf was approximately three feet from her body and contained a bloody fingerprint. He went onto say he had sent the leaf to the F.B.I. Laboratory in Washington, D.C. for fingerprint analysis. He showed where he and Police Officer Jack Potter had signed their initials before sealing the box that contained the table leaf. The box, he explained, remained sealed. Defense attorney Griffin objected to the evidence being placed before the jury, citing there was no way of knowing if it had been tampered with. Judge Rosellini ruled that it would not be admissible until that time that F.B.I. agents testified about their findings at the crime laboratory. The leaf was eventually shown to the jury.

The jury of ten men and two women heard from Fanny's neighbors. They testified about their system of letting one another know they were all right. They spoke of finding Fanny's body in her laundry room. Other neighbors testified to seeing Carl near Fanny's house the afternoon of the murder.

Police Officer Jack Nash and Detective Carl Petersen told the jury about arriving at the crime scene and investigating the homicide. Detective Petersen described the two-year journey to return Carl to America. He testified about finally being able to go to Gothenburg, Sweden, and retrieving his prisoner. Tacoma Police Identification Assistant Charles Marsh showed the jury photographs from the crime scene. When the graphic photographs were shown, Carl turned away and did not look at them.

A taxicab driver told the jury he took Carl to a tavern the day prior to the murder. At the tavern, Carl purchased five cigars, according to the taxicab driver. He testified he drove Carl to the railroad station in Tacoma on the day the murder took place. A baggage clerk, Malcolm Wood, testified he checked Carl's luggage at the Tacoma train station at approximately 5:20 p.m. on the day of the murder.

F.B.I. Agent Sebastin Latona told the jury it was his "conclusive opinion" the fingerprints found at the crime scene belonged to Carl.

Carl's uncle from Renton took the witness stand and informed the court Carl was with him on the evening in question. He explained they played pinocle with some of his friends. Later, he said, they played Norwegian card games. It was his testimony Carl stayed with him until he left for Norway, a trip that the uncle paid for. Carl's aunt backed up the testimony stating Carl was with them in Renton when Fanny was killed.

A retired fingerprint expert, A. C. Rosenfelt, testified on behalf of the defense team. It was his testimony that the fingerprints were too bloody for any comparison work to be done.

On the final day of the murder trial, Carl took the witness stand. A translator was used during his testimony. He emphatically stated he had nothing to do with the murder. He added he had only had one conversation with Fanny, and that was months before she was murdered.

Tracy asked, "Where did you meet her?"

Carl answered, "At her residence."

Tracy then asked, "Was that the only time you were in her house?"

Carl quickly answered, "Yes."

His attorney then asked, "Did you see her again?"

Carl stated, "Well, I can't answer that. Possibly not. He explained that he might have seen her on the street, but they did not speak."

With that explanation, Tracy asked, "Were you in her house on or about October 11, 1950?"

Without a moment of hesitation, Carl replied, "No."

Tracy quickly asked, "Did you kill Mrs. Rice?"

Carl stated, "No."

Tracy's last question was, "When did you first hear of her death?"

Carl simply said, "From the police in Sweden."

Carl added he was visiting his aunt and uncle in Renton at the time Fanny was murdered. He expanded on the testimony saying he took a bus from Seattle to Tacoma, then took a taxi to his relative's house.

The jury deliberated for thirteen hours before returning a verdict of guilty of first-degree murder. The jury did not recommend the death penalty. Carl was sentenced to life in prison. Prosecutor O'Connell and Judge Rosellini recommended the minimum prison sentence. At the time Carl was sentenced in 1953, the minimum sentence was thirteen years and four months. As the guards escorted Carl back to the Pierce County jail, a reporter asked, "Have you anything to say to the people of Norway?" Without hesitating, Carl replied, "No, I have nothing to say. Now I must submit to my fate."

Carl's defense team filed a notice of appeal with the State Supreme Court. Days later they withdrew the appeal. Carl was transported to the Walla Walla prison to begin his life sentence. He was thirty-seven years old when the prison doors clanged shut. Carl was paroled on October 27, 1970, and deported to his homeland of Holmstrand, Norway.

8
A MYSTERY IN LONGVIEW

Eight-year-old Rima Traxler was last seen walking home from St. Helens Elementary School in Longview on May 15, 1985. She was wearing a tan plaid skirt, a pink shirt, and a tan knee-length coat when she disappeared. She was approximately 4 feet tall, weighed 45–50 pounds, and had long blonde hair and blue eyes. Rima was born on November 9, 1976.

When she did not arrive home, the Longview Police Department was brought in. They called in neighboring police agencies, the Civil Air Patrol, the Tri-County Search and Rescue, and the Cowlitz County Sheriff's Office. More than 100 officers, along with bloodhounds and German shepherds searched all night for Rima without any results. Officers made contact with all of Rima's classmates but no one had any answers as to what happened to the second grader.

Her mother, Danelle, told reporters she became concerned when Rima did not arrive home an hour after school got out. "She usually comes straight home from school. When I walked to the school yesterday, I had a feeling she was gone." Rima had a five-year-old brother. Danelle was in the process of divorcing her husband, Rima's stepfather. Rima's biological father lived in Alaska. Rima had not seen her father in years. He was quickly ruled out as a suspect after the police contacted him.

Danelle told reporters:

For the last four years she's had drills on what to do if someone tries to grab her. We even have a code word if a stranger tries to come up to her. If she ran away, it was because she was hanging around with older kids.[1]

Danelle said Rima liked to play with Barbie dolls and draw unicorns. She described Rima as a "smart, independent" girl. She said Rima was "a momma's girl." She added that Rima liked to go to church, wear dresses, and have her hair braided in French braids or have her hair pulled into a ponytail on the side of her head. She added, "I just hope they find her. And I hope she's OK."

One classmate told the police Rima said she was going home. Another classmate remembered seeing Rima walking in the opposite direction of her home. Several children told the investigators a car drove by the playground when they were at recess during lunch. Some of the children remembered hearing a passenger in the car yell out, "We'll see you after school, girls," but others said that was not true. One child said she saw Rima get into a green car with an Oregon license plate, but soon retracted her statement.

The next day, hundreds of searchers went door-to-door trying to locate Rima. They were assisted by fifty students from R.A. Long High School. Longview Police Department Lieutenant Hal Mahnke told reporter Linda Wilson of the *Longview Daily News* "Right now there aren't any real substantial leads. But we're working on every little piece of information we've got."

Days turned into weeks and Detective Sergeant Charlie Harper told the media, "We are just going to keep plugging away, hoping for a break." Other agencies that helped the Longview Police Department included the Cowlitz County Sheriff's Office, Kelso Police Department, Longview Police Reserves, Cowlitz County Sheriff's Office Cadets, Cowlitz County Sheriff's Posse, Cowlitz County Sheriff's Divers, Cowlitz County Department of Emergency Services, Longview Sanitation Department, Tri-County Search and Rescue, Pacific County Search and Rescue, Lower Columbia Amateur Radio Association, Sea Explorers, Northwest Bloodhounds Association, Civil Air Patrol, Longview School District, the Salvation Army, and citizen volunteers.

A fund was set up named "Help Find Rima Fund." The fund was used for producing flyers and covering the expense of postage. A block ad ran in the *Longview Daily News* with Rima's photo, with the heading: "Where's Rima?"

Soon after Rima disappeared, Quality Inns International, AT&T, and Outdoor Advertising teamed up to cover 5,000 billboards across America with posters of missing children. The National Center for Missing and Exploited Children provided the information for the billboards. Rima's information was included for the new billboard project. Quality Inns International placed pictures of missing children and provided a special telephone in their lobbies that connected directly with the National Center for Missing and Exploited Children.

Rima's photo and information appeared on the back of a Cheerios box. She was featured in a missing child ad for *Sports Illustrated Magazine*, local real estate magazines, as well as the new billboard campaign. An organization, Kids Missing in America, out of California, placed Rima's picture on copper bracelets they sold to benefit the National Child Safety Council.

When there were no easy answers forthcoming, Danelle told the press that until Rima's body was located, she would continue to believe someone had her daughter:

> I just hope they don't hurt her and that they'll bring her back. Whoever's got my daughter, please, bring her back.... Some crazy person took her. Why would someone take someone else's child? I'm not going to give up until I find her.

At the one-year anniversary of Rima's disappearance, Danelle voiced her frustration with the case:

> Time hasn't made the hurt less. I go to the store to buy clothes for my son, and I see these cute little things I know she'd like, and it makes me sad. I sit and think about Rima. I get angry, and I cry, and it hurts just as much as it did the day she disappeared.

For Rima's ninth birthday, she bought her daughter a necklace with butterflies in the hopes she would be home to open the gift.

On the second anniversary of Rima's disappearance, Lieutenant Charlie Harper, who had been on the case from the beginning as the Detective Sergeant, told the media:

> I believe there is a person or persons who have information, and for some reason they have not come forward. The case will never be closed unless there's some type of solution or answers. We don't forget about missing little girls.

Lieutenant Harper was referring to the unsolved murder of eight-year-old Chila Silvernails. On the morning of April 20, 1982, Chila walked out of the family home to wait for the school bus, but when the bus arrived, Chila was nowhere in sight. Her lunch pail was still sitting at the end of the driveway where she would have boarded the school bus. Chila never made it to school. She was reported missing and law enforcement worked around the clock to locate her.

A witness reported seeing a white over blue two-door vehicle approximately two blocks from her house. The car was heading down the street towards where Chila would have been standing at the end of her driveway waiting to board her school bus that would take her to the Kalama Elementary School. The witness said the male driver was alone in the car. Other witnesses came forward after recalling seeing the vehicle in the area. A description of the driver was broadcast to the public and a composite sketch was created.

The following day, Chila's body was located in a creek near Shirley Gordon Road, south of Kalama. The autopsy showed the child had been stabbed in the throat and asphyxiated. The knife was never recovered. Many tips came in; suspects were developed, but later eliminated. Chief Criminal Deputy Gary Lee told the press, "We've felt we were close several times, but that guy is still out there somewhere."

Cowlitz County Sheriff Les Nelson told the media, "One thing I will tell you, is that we won't rest until we get the individual responsible for that little girl's death."

Forty years later, the Cowlitz County Sheriff's Office is still actively working on the Chila Silvernails case. They are asking if anyone has any information to please contact them at 360-577-3092.

When yet another child went missing from Longview, it only added to the complicated investigation. Kara Patricia Rudd, age twelve, was last seen leaving school on November 21, 1996, walking towards a gold-colored 1982 Pontiac Firebird. Minutes later, she exited the car. Kara was a sixth-grader at Monticello Middle School. Her mother, Janet, reported her missing when she did not return home after school.

Kara was born in Olympia and moved to Longview at the age of six months. She had one sister. Kara's nickname was "Hug-A-Bug" for her love of all bugs—except spiders. She loved all animals and enjoyed music, dancing, camping, roller skating, and swimming. A reporter questioned one of Kara's relatives about the possibility that perhaps Kara ran away from home. In response, the relative replied:

> She had nothing to run away from. I'm really hopeful because I know we're going to find her, but I'm starting to get a little worried. It's been a real long time, and she hasn't called. It's not like Kara to worry her mom like that. I'm praying she's just a runaway, but myself, [I think] she wouldn't do that. She would have called me, or her sister, or her mom.[2]

As the Cowlitz County Sheriff's Office scoured the area with the help of other law enforcement agencies and the National Guard, the detectives developed a possible suspect. Their investigation revealed a friend of the family, Joseph Robert Kondro, had been living in the Rudd's garage. The investigators learned Joseph allegedly asked his ex-wife not to cooperate with the investigation into Kara's disappearance. After this information came to light, Joseph was arrested for tampering with a witness.

The local newspaper reported the Longview Police Department arrested Joseph in connection with the disappearance of Kara Rudd. Soon after, a nine-year-old girl came forward and told the investigators Joseph had touched her inappropriately the previous summer. Days later, a seven-year-old girl came forward and reported the same thing. Soon after a ten-year-old girl told detectives with the Longview Police Department that Joseph raped her in June 1992. All of the children knew Joseph through their parents. Joseph was charged with rape and child molestation.

Six weeks after Kara was last seen alive, her body was located underneath an abandoned car on Mount Solo. Due to the decomposition of the body, Kara was identified by dental records and the remnants of her clothing. The authorities determined Kara had been raped prior to being murdered. Kara, who played an angel in a Christmas pageant when she was ten years old, was laid to rest after a service that was attended by nearly 400 people.

Two weeks later, Joseph was charged with aggravated first-degree murder. The investigation revealed that Joseph was a friend of Rima's stepfather when he was married to Rima's mother. This information renewed the search for Rima's body. A search party combed the area of Mount Solo with bloodhounds trained to detect human remains but did not have any success. Longview Police Detective Scott McDaniel contacted the Russian Embassy requesting their satellite imaging.

Joseph confessed to raping and murdering both Kara and Rima. Joseph passed three voice stress analysis tests during which he admitted to both murders. Additionally, he accurately described an article of clothing that Rima was wearing when she was murdered. The article of clothing had never been made public. He admitted he came across Rima when she was walking home from school. He told the investigators he gave her the family's secret word "Unicorn," which meant it was okay for her to get into his car. He said he told Rima her mother and stepfather wanted him to take her to a swimming hole, where they would meet them later that afternoon.

During his confession, Joseph admitted he drove to Kara's school. He said she got into his car briefly before returning to school. He said they arranged to meet at a nearby lake. Joseph admitted he took Kara to an abandoned house where he raped and strangled her. He told the investigators he then placed Kara's body in his car and drove to Mount Solo, where he placed her body under an abandoned Volkswagen.

Joseph pled guilty to first-degree murder for Kara and second-degree intentional murder for Rima. During the court proceeding, Joseph read a prepared statement:

On or about November 21, 1996, I did intentionally restrain, abduct or kidnap Kara Rudd by transporting her in my car to an abandoned building located in Cowlitz County ... I committed the act of kidnapping Kara Rudd with the intent to inflict bodily injury upon her ... I did in fact cause her death by means of strangulation.[3]

When asked, he admitted he raped Kara. Joseph went onto say, "On or about May 15, 1985 I did with intent to cause the death by means of strangulation," referring to the murder of Rima. Joseph admitted he hid Rima's body in a creek in Cowlitz County.

Despite numerous searches, Rima's body was never located. Joseph was taken to the area where he said he hid Rima's body underneath a log before covering it with brush. Detective McDaniel explained that due to the fact Rima was apparently not buried, and that the creek had flooded its banks and changed course over the years, it was unlikely anything would be left where Joseph said it was.

Joseph was convicted of rape and molestation on the other cases. He received a sentence of fourteen years in prison for the other cases. He received a sentence of fifty-five years for the two murders. Under the plea agreement, Joseph forfeited his rights to appeal any of the cases.

Kara's mother told reporters, "If we wouldn't have made the decision to go ahead with the deal, we wouldn't have known about Rima ... Rima was everybody's girl after so long." After the court proceeding, Rima's mother told reporter Laurie Smith of the *Longview Daily News*:

Even though this is not the outcome I had hoped, prayed and dreamed for, it is an answer. But with it comes so many more questions and heartaches. All of my hopes, prayers, and dreams have been in vain, for my worst fear has come to be a reality. I have been waiting 14 years for answers, yet to finally have answers does not ease the pain....[4]

The investigators were never able to tie Joseph to Chila's murder or any other murder, although they believed there could have been additional victims. Joseph died in the Walla Walla prison in 2012 from natural causes.

9

JO ANN DEWEY

The residents of the Central Court Apartments in Vancouver heard a woman screaming at approximately 11:30 p.m. on Sunday, March 19, 1950. One resident ran outside when he heard the woman screaming and saw a man picking up "what looked like a woman's jacket about 20 feet east of a car." He asked the man what was happening, to which he got a stern reply, "shut up, it's my wife." He heard the woman shout that she was not his wife just before they drove off. The resident did not think anything more of it and assumed it was a domestic argument. One woman who saw the commotion from a distance was bothered enough by what she saw, to contact the local police. When they arrived on scene, they found a quiet street with nothing out of the ordinary.

The following morning at 10:10 a.m., Jo Ann Dewey's mother walked into the Clark County Sheriff's Office and reported her eighteen-year-old daughter missing. Jo Ann was described as 5 feet 4 inches with curly brown hair and bangs. Her mother said she had a small scar on her face. When she was last seen, she was a wearing a rust-colored coat over a blue skirt and a white blouse, with white bobby socks and brown loafers.

Jo Ann's mother explained to the deputies that Jo Ann worked at the Portland Sanitarium and arrived in Vancouver by bus Sunday night at approximately 11 p.m. Jo Ann intended to spend some time with her family in Battle Ground before returning home. Her mother was working an overnight shift at a nursing home so she asked Jo Ann to walk a few blocks to St. Joseph's Hospital and stay there with a friend of the family until she could come and get her.

When Jo Ann's mother arrived at the hospital, she learned her daughter never arrived. The Clark County Sheriff's Office notified the Vancouver Police Department and officers began canvassing the area Jo Ann would have walked. They located a broken purse handle and a hair barrette, near Thirteenth and D Streets where residents of the Central Court Apartments recalled hearing a woman screaming the night before.

The Clark County Sheriff Office notified all neighboring law enforcement agencies. Law enforcement bulletins were created and distributed throughout Washington and Oregon.

The case was similar to one the Washington State Patrol worked one week before. In that case, a young woman flagged down a passing motorist at Thirteenth and Broadway Streets on a Sunday at approximately 11:30 p.m. and asked them to notify the Washington State Patrol that two or three men attacked her. When law enforcement arrived in the area, the woman was nowhere to be found. They were unable to get any further information from witnesses.

Vancouver Police Chief Harry Diamond held a press conference and asked the woman to come forward with additional information. He believed the two cases were related. Jo Ann's mother also made a plea to the public for any assistance in locating her daughter. She added, "It's just not safe for girls to be out alone anymore and I think my daughter's disappearance should be an object lesson to all parents."

A few people came forward and reported they had seen a woman struggling with two men while screaming Sunday at approximately 11:30 p.m. but they were unable to give a description of either man due to the poor lighting on the street. Later that week, Vancouver Mayor Vern Anderson was asked to approve funds for better lighting.

Deputies and detectives with the Clark County Sheriff's Office worked all night searching the nearby wooded area and heavily dense brush but to no avail. The next morning, the Vancouver Police Department split their officers and detectives into two squads of ten each to search the wooded areas.

The following day, Police Chief Diamond admitted they were at a "dead end." He asked the public to continue to provide tips but said they had exhausted all leads provided thus far. He said law enforcement had searched parks, ravines, water holes, rivers, lakes and the shores surrounding them. Police Chief Diamond added he was sending a group of ten police reserve officers to search an area of some new construction in town. Additionally, he asked his police officers to search all isolated areas on their beats. The public was asked to search any outbuildings on their properties. Farmers and ranchers were asked to search their land.

Police Chief Diamond requested that all available men in Clark County volunteer their time Saturday, March 25, 1950, for an "all-out search." He mentioned he would be requesting assistance from the local horse clubs to search the more rugged terrain. Police Chief Diamond asked:

Those volunteers who want to take part must wear old clothes because some of the area to be covered is rough and brushy. We are asking, too, that as many as can bring cars or trucks, as we are short of transportation.

Police Chief Diamond, Clark County Sheriff Earl Anderson, and Washington State Patrol Sergeant James Coshow worked together to map out the areas to be searched by each group. All available police reserve officers were asked to report for duty on Saturday and Sunday to aid the search teams. Some 500 volunteers reported for duty on Saturday morning. They were broken into groups headed by a law enforcement officer to begin the intensive search. The officers were equipped with walkie-talkie radios to maintain contact.

As it turned out, the search parties were unable to locate Jo Ann. However, on Sunday morning, a group of fishermen discovered Jo Ann's nude body on a sand bar in Wind River in Skamania County, sixty miles from where she had been abducted. Her body was badly beaten when it was located by Bob Rummel, age twenty-four, Gerald Frandle, age twenty-five, and Ray Lowry, age twenty-seven:

Suddenly we spied a dark object in the rocks of that gravel bar out in the middle. I don't know which one of us saw it first–maybe all three of us at once. It looked like a body. The closer we got to the shore and the more we talked about it, the more we thought it was a body.

When we got to the bank, we waded out to the gravel bar, to see for sure what the object was. Sure enough, it was the body of a girl. She was lying face down, in about six inches of water at the time.[1]

The trio immediately thought of the Jo Ann Dewey case they had read about in newspapers. They hiked a quarter of a mile to the St. Martin's Hot Springs Hotel. They relayed their information to the hotel manager, Arthur McCoy. He in turn phoned Skamania County Sheriff Jim Read. Sheriff Read along with Clark County Sheriff Anderson and Chief Criminal Deputy Arthur Swick drove to the river. They crossed over a footbridge to where they could see the body. Sheriff Anderson said he "knew right away it was Jo Ann, by the scar on the right cheek and the similarity to the many pictures I had seen."

Washington State Police Patrolman Harold Cusic arrived on scene and was able to positively identify Jo Ann because he knew her prior to her abduction. Skamania County Prosecutor/Coroner Ray Sly drove to the crime scene and immediately called for a coroner's jury. A jury was assembled on the riverbank. The three fishermen told their stories in front of the coroner's jury as the rain poured down along the river.

Skamania County Sheriff Jim Reed gathered a group of searchers which included deputies from Clark County and Skamania County, Washington State Patrol, Vancouver Police Department, citizen volunteers, and county officials. Their first task was to search the nearby woods for any trace of Jo Ann's clothing. They were also asked to search all empty cabins, abandoned outbuildings, all pathways, and trails in the vicinity.

Washington State Patrol Don Drake along with five Vancouver police officers, ten Vancouver Fire Department volunteers, and two of Jo Ann's brothers began sifting through the ashes of an abandoned old shack that burned mysteriously four days prior to the discovery of Jo Ann's body. They seized small pieces of cloth for analysis. Other law enforcement officers were sent to a nearby dump to search for evidence. Forty officers searched a 15-mile range from where the body was located, but did not locate anything of significance. Those living nearby were questioned but no one recalled seeing anything out of the ordinary.

The day after Jo Ann was laid to rest, arrest warrants were issued for Truman G. Wilson, age twenty-four, and his brother Utah E. Wilson, age twenty-one. The brothers had been in trouble with the law since they were juveniles. Their two older brothers were serving time at the Oregon State Penitentiary when the arrest warrants were signed for Truman and Utah. Another older brother, Grant, was the person who contacted the authorities and told them Utah and Truman were responsible for the homicide. Grant had never been in trouble with the law.

Truman's criminal history included burglary, assault and rape. He escaped from the Oregon State Penitentiary while serving seven years for rape. He was recaptured and returned to the Oregon State Penitentiary. He also served time for armed robbery and assault. Utah's first brush with the law was as a juvenile. He was sent to a training school but escaped before being recaptured.

The police in Portland came across an abandoned car that belonged to the Wilson's brother. Inside the car they located a small piece of either a bone or a tooth, a button, human hair, blood, and a label from a beer bottle. At the scene of the abduction, the police located a beer bottle. The bottle was tested for fingerprints by the Portland Police Bureau who believed the prints were Utah Wilson's. The Portland Police Bureau planned to send the beer bottle to the F.B.I. Laboratory in Washington, D.C. Another car believed to have been driven by either Utah or Truman was turned over to the Vancouver Police Department after being located in Camas.

While the Vancouver detectives were analyzing both vehicles, officers with the Sacramento (California) Police Department located Truman and Utah. They were placed in separate jail cells where they repeatedly said they had nothing to do with the kidnapping and homicide. They waived extradition and waited to be returned to Washington.

While waiting for Police Chief Diamond and Sheriff Anderson, the brothers agreed to talk with a group of reporters. Truman began by explaining that one of their two older brothers was a suspect in the theft of a power saw. The only reason they left Vancouver, Truman explained, was to protect Utah, who was on parole. Utah told the reporters they left Washington to go on a "joy ride." When the reporters asked about the night in question, Utah refused to say anything; Truman said he needed to consult an attorney.

Detective Robert Doyle of the Sacramento Police Department informed the reporters that Utah told him he was near the area of the abduction, but added, "I don't know anything about it except what I read in the newspapers."

Utah's seventeen-year-old wife, Lucille Cline, told the reporters, "I'll stick by Utah until I find out what the outcome is going to be." The couple had only been married four months and his wife said it was a "complete surprise" to her when she found out he had been arrested for murder. When she was asked by the reporters about her husband's whereabouts on the night of the abduction, she replied, "I don't know where they were the night she was abducted. They told me they were going to Silverton (Oregon)—yeah, to see their father." She expressed her disappointment that her last name had been misspelled in the newspaper the previous day by saying, "My name is Cline with a C and not a K like it was in the papers. I don't mind making the front pages, but I'd like to have my name spelled right." She explained a possible reason for blood being in her husband's car was that he could have hit a dog and placed it in the car. She did say Utah had not been able to find a job and mainly spent his days fishing.

Utah and Truman's mother made a strong statement by saying, "I just know that my sons are not guilty. I feel it in my heart." She added, "The boys' record [sic.] are being held against them." Utah's mother-in-law also held steadfast that Utah could not be involved in the murder.

A decision was made to exhume Jo Ann's body just long enough to get her fingerprints in an effort to determine if her fingerprints could be located on or inside the car.

"One jail is as good as another," lamented Utah after being transported from Sacramento to Cowlitz County jail as he sat in a jail cell chain smoking and reading a detective magazine. Cowlitz County Sheriff C. W. Reynolds told the reporters Truman had "exploded" in his jail cell yelling that he was not guilty and that he "will sue everyone connected with linking me with the case."

Truman and Utah pled innocent to the charge of kidnapping and murder. Their trial opened three months after the murder with Judge Eugene Cushing presiding. The jury consisted of four woman and eight men. When a juror had to leave unexpectedly, the deputies went outside and found six people on the street and brought them back into the courtroom. One of the six was selected as an alternate.

The brother's defense attorneys, Irvin Goodman and Sanford Clement, accused the prosecution of planting an eavesdropping device in the jail cell Truman and Utah shared. Cowlitz County District Attorney DeWitt Jones denied such an action. The defense stressed to the court that Truman and Utah were watching a double-feature movie at the Playhouse Theater in Portland on the night Jo Ann was abducted and murdered.

Grant took the witness stand and told the jury his brothers had been the victims of harassment by law enforcement. That was the reason, they had to leave the state of Washington, according to Grant. He emphasized their decision to leave the state had nothing to do with the homicide. Grant admitted to telling the Vancouver police where they could locate his brothers in Sacramento. He explained he was the registered owner of both of the cars the police seized, but he admitted Truman and Utah had keys to both cars. Grant emphasized that neither car had been driven for at least a week before he sold them.

Oregon State Police Criminologist Dr. Howard Richardson, testified that Jo Ann had been sexually assaulted and beaten by someone's fists prior to dying from carbon monoxide poison. It was Dr. Richardson's belief that Jo Ann was placed in the trunk or back seat of the car she was pulled into. Additionally, two hairs located in the trunk appeared to be of the same texture as Jo Ann's. The jurors learned Grant sold the car in question the day after Jo Ann's body was found.

A fingerprint expert from the F.B.I., Edwin Dius, told the panel of jurors it was his "positive conclusion" that the fingerprints on the beer bottle found at the abduction site belonged to Utah. Under cross-examination, he admitted he was unable to determine how old the fingerprints on the bottle were.

The jury heard from F.B.I. agents, Guy Tull and James Tanner. They explained the brothers had used fictious names when they registered at a motel in Sacramento. Police Chief Diamond told the court that the woman who initially contacted them after hearing a female screaming, selected Truman and Utah out of a police lineup. He further explained that the woman lived at the Central Court Apartments. She described seeing a man of medium build, wearing a gray suit with dark slick hair, beating a woman. Police Chief Diamond also told the jury on the drive from California to Washington, "Utah choked up and started sobbing. One time he broke down and cried."

Deputies had to turn away seventy-five potential spectators the morning Truman and Utah's mother, Eunice Wilson, took the witness stand. She told the court she gave Grant $1,000 to give to Truman and Utah. It was not for them to leave the state, she explained, but instead, it was money Truman had given her from his paychecks and for Utah to take a vacation.

All eyes were on Truman when he took the witness stand. He testified that he and his brother were at a theater in Portland when Jo Ann was killed. He elaborated saying they left the theater just after midnight, and stopped for cigarettes on the way home. They had trouble getting the car started when they left the store, he said, but eventually they were able to drive home. As they approached their mother's house, Truman explained, they saw three cars they presumed were police cars. They decided to drive to Grant's house and switch out cars. The reason he gave for this was "in case the cars were police cars" they didn't want to drive past their mother's house twice in the same car. He emphasized they did not want to be "conspicuous" in case the police were looking for Utah. The judge would not allow them to mention the theft of the power saw as a reason why the police were looking for Utah.

Prosecutor Jones honed in on the reason for switching out the cars. He asked Truman, "You didn't think, did you that they were looking for a black colored Buick?" Truman replied they did not know what type of car the police were looking for, but explained, "If they were police cars and we drove up and down in the Buick the police would know we were coming home."

When Prosecutor Jones asked, "Why did you think the police would be watching your mother's home?" Truman quickly stated, "I didn't say that. I said I thought they were watching my mother's place."

Truman testified that after switching out the cars, they went to Utah's house because he wanted to see his wife. They waited in their car for a period of time to see if any police cars came by. When they determined there were no police cars in the vicinity, they went inside Utah's house briefly before heading back to Grant's house. They told Grant they feared the police were looking for Utah regarding the stolen power saw. They only stayed at his house a few minutes before going to their mother's house. They left there after a few minutes and went to a store to buy hot dogs and milk before heading to Lackamas Lake, where they slept in their car.

Truman went onto explain that Grant met up with them and gave them the money introduced into evidence. When they left the lake, they headed to their father's trailer in Silverton. From there they headed to Medford, Oregon, where they spent three days at the Carlyle Hotel. They returned to Silverton before driving back to Grant's house briefly before driving to

Sacramento. Prosecutor Jones asked why they went to Medford. Truman's answer was to look for work, but upon further questioning he admitted neither of them ever applied for any jobs in Medford. Truman said they wanted to speak to a friend who lived at the Allen Hotel in Medford regarding a job but admitted they never contacted him.

When the prosecution questioned Truman about using fictitious names, he replied that he preferred doing so because "his name had been splashed in the newspapers." He confirmed he did not expect to be arrested in California. Prosecutor Jones confronted Truman with a statement he allegedly made to a reporter in California. From the witness stand, Truman denied ever saying, "if we had known the police were looking for us we wouldn't have been here." Truman elaborated by saying what he meant to say was if they had known the police were looking for them, they would have turned themselves in.

Utah took the witness stand and confirmed their activities the night Jo Ann was murdered adding that they watched two movies that night; "Captain Fury" and "Captain Courageous." Utah told of their activities in the week following the homicide. He told the court his criminal history included breaking into taverns in Clark County. He was released from jail, he said, two months prior to marrying his wife, Lucille. He admitted he was not employed because he "couldn't seem to find a job."

Alluding to the fingerprints found on the beer bottle, Utah was asked how he generally disposed of his empty beer bottles. His response ranged from tossing them out a car window, leaving them by a curb, leaving them in a vacant lot by his mother-in-law's house, or placing them in the garbage can at his mother-in-law's house where he and Lucille lived. He stressed he did not know how his fingerprints got on the beer bottle that was in possession of the police.

Before the defense rested, they called Betty Lyon to the witness stand. Betty told the jury she worked as an usherette at the movie theater where the brothers were on the night in question, March 19, 1950. Betty explained she only worked at the movie theater one night; the night of the abduction. Under cross-examination, Betty admitted she was not able to recall the exact date when questioned previously by a detective. When asked to produce a pay stub for that night, Betty said she had not been able to locate her pay stub.

The prosecution then called two law enforcement officers who testified Betty told them she did not work at the theater on March 19. The manager of the movie theater, Robert Butts, took the witness stand. He told the panel of jurists his records showed Betty worked on March 22, not March 19.

By the time closing arguments began, the trail had lasted seventeen days; longer than any murder trial in Clark County's history up to that time.

The state began by reminding the jurors that an F.B.I. agent testified Utah's fingerprints were on the beer bottle found at the site of the abduction. Prosecutor Jones referred to the fingerprints as better evidence than if "fifty people had stood there and seen the crime." He explained:

> Identification by another person can sometimes be erroneous, and not nearly as important as the positive identification that are on the pads of each finger of each person's hands. This is the one calling card that God has equipped each individual with that no one in this world can duplicate.
>
> The person who was at the wheel of that car threw out that bottle. That bottle was found in the street on the driver's side and it had live beer in it.[2]

Prosecutor Jones reminded the jurors that the woman who saw a man beating a woman in front of the Central Court Apartments wore a gray suit and had dark, slick hair: "I say to you that Truman has dark slick hair, and is of medium build and he came to court wearing a gray suit at one time during this trial."

The prosecutor reminded the jurors the brothers feared the police were waiting for him near his mother's house on the night of the abduction, and that Grant sold the automobile soon after Jo Ann's body was located. He pointed out that even if Truman and Utah had been at the Playhouse Theater at 9 p.m. on the night of March 19, they would still have had time to commit the crime that night.

Prosecutor Jones said it was fortunate that so much evidence was left behind and they could prosecute Truman and Utah, saying, "For next time they [may] be more careful—they may leave no evidence behind." In conclusion the prosecutor said, "I was astounded in this case at the amount of evidence that was available to be put before you. All this evidence points up the knowledge of guilt—it is inconsistent with innocence."[3]

Defense Attorney Goodman emphasized that the state never made their case. He questioned if the man who heard a scream was correct in what type of vehicle they pushed the woman into. He described the woman who picked Truman and Utah out of a police lineup as "confused." He added, "I think Mrs. Nelson is a very fine person but I think she is a very confused person." He pointed out that her testimony was that she was reading the newspaper in bed when she heard a female scream. "You can't read a newspaper without a light being on. There was no evidence in this case that light was ever turned off."

Before Defense Attorney Goodman finished his closing remarks, he stated:

The men who destroyed that human life will be apprehended and removed. If in the meantime, these boys die on the gallows, Detective Borgan can square the role he has played with his own conscience. This same statement applies to Detective Ulmer.

He informed the jury the two police officers "had something to do with that beer bottle," before adding that they "were very, very deep in the case."[4]

In conclusion, Defense Attorney Goodman told the jury, "When I sit down, the fate of Utah and Truman Wilson will rest with you—whether they live or die."

With that, Judge Cushing gave the jury their instructions and explained what their options were as to the guilt or innocence of the two brothers. It only took the jury five hours to return a verdict of guilty of kidnapping and first-degree murder for both Truman and Utah. Utah's wife ran out of the courtroom sobbing as soon as the verdict was read. Judge Cushing ordered that Truman and Utah die by hanging for the kidnapping and murder of Jo Ann Dewey. The following day, Defense Attorney Goodman began the process for requesting a new trial.

Before Defense Attorney Goodman finished the appeals, he notified the police that he had received a hand written letter wherein the writer confessed to the crime. The writer mentioned where the authorities could find Jo Ann's ring and "other things." Prosecutor Jones referred to the letter as a "crank."

Judge Cushing denied the defense's request for a new trial and the case headed for the Washington Supreme Court. As the appeal process was underway, the defense's accusation that the prosecution planted a listening device in the Wilson's jail cell came to light.

Clark County Sheriff Anderson confirmed the defense's suspicions that the jail cell was wired for a listening device that was hidden in the ventilation system. The conversations between Truman and Utah were not only recorded, they were also transcribed. After the accusation was made on the first day of the trial, the brothers were moved to separate jail cells for the remainder of the trial. Sheriff Anderson requested $1,700 from the Clark County Commissioners to cover the expense of the wiretapping. In a letter he requested: $550 for office supplies, $500 for office equipment, $550 for special services, and $100 for a telephone and telegraph line.

The Clark County Commissioners approved the expense and directed the funds be taken out of the jail grocery budget, the mileage account, and the clothing budget. Months later, they approved an emergency appropriation for $5,500 to cover the overage expenses for the trial.

As the Wilson brothers were waiting their fate on the gallows, they helped thwart a jail escape. Sheriff Anderson later told reporters:

> At 12:30 a.m. three teenage prisoners held on grand larceny charges flooded their cell with water, a jailer came to investigate and they overpowered him and took his keys.
>
> The three then unlocked the cells in which the Wilson brothers were held, then broke into the commissary and the property room, picking up some clothing and a small amount of cash.
>
> While they were doing that, Utah Wilson walked into the kitchen, picking up a meat cleaver and some knives. Then he woke up two trusties and told them of the jail-break attempt. Joining forces, the trusties and the Wilsons forced the three back into their cell.[5]

Sheriff Anderson added that Truman used the inter-office phone and called the deputy on duty downstairs and informed him of the escape attempt.

Just before the calendar clicked over to 1951, the Washington Supreme Court agreed to hear the case. The nine supreme court justices denied the appeal, basing their denial on the beer bottle. Justice Matthew Hill wrote:

> Although no one positively identified Truman and Utah as the men who had seized Jo Ann Dewey and driven away with her, Utah's fingerprints on the recently opened beer bottle afford an identification that completely disposes of appellants' contention that there was in Clark County at the time of the kidnapping.
>
> It seems to us that Utah's fingerprints on the recently opened beer bottle–is the most conclusive evidence of his presence at that time and place that could be offered.[6]

After their appeal was denied, Truman and Utah appeared before Judge Cushing who set an execution date of August 20, 1951. An appeal was filed with the U.S. Supreme Court and the execution was postponed until November 30, 1951. Hours before they were to hang, the brothers received a short stay from the U.S. Ninth Circuit Court of Appeals. They set the execution date as December 3, 1951, or "to such time that the supreme court of the United States, or a justice thereof, shall direct."

When Truman heard the news, he was overheard saying, "This gives us a chance. A little more time. Now if we can only get an honest investigation." Washington State Governor Arthur Langlie, who had denied the Wilsons executive clemency the day before, announced he was "prepared to seriously review" information provided by former Clark County Deputy Sheriff Howard Hanson, who believed the Wilsons had been wrongly convicted.

Yet again, with hours to spare, the U.S. Supreme Court granted a stay of execution pending the appropriate filing and disposition of petitions. The defense team announced they had enough new evidence to warrant a new trial. They asked Governor Langlie to commute the Wilson's sentence to life imprisonment, but he denied the request.

The year 1952 saw more appeals and delays. Governor Langlie appointed a committee consisting of three nationally recognized attorneys to review the case. The committee consisted of Harlan S. Don Carlos of Hartford, Connecticut; Henry Franklin of Peterborough, New Hampshire; and Erle Stanley Gardner of Temecula, California.

The committee found "no doubt" as to Truman's guilt in the kidnapping and murder of Jo Ann Dewey. They found Utah may not have participated in the actual abduction and homicide, but he was quite possibly an accessory after the fact. At a minimum, Utah had knowledge of the crime, the committee concluded.

One item the committee concentrated on was the recordings that took place in the jail cell. The committee decided because the Wilsons had been warned their conversations might be recorded; no crime was committed. After reviewing the case, the committee concluded:

> It was Utah Wilson's fingerprints which were found on the beer bottle. This, the committee found, represents a piece of genuine evidence. It is Utah himself who testified, and continues to assert, that he was with Truman at all times on the night the crime was committed. It is Utah's alibi, as well as Truman's, which was thoroughly discredited.

After reviewing the committee's findings, Governor Langlie wrote:

> The Wilson brothers now stand convicted of murder. They are no longer entitled to the presumption of innocence. In fact, the presumption now is that they are guilty.
>
> Neither of them has done anything to overcome that presumption. On the contrary, they have, as the committee found, impeded the investigation by their persistent refusal to tell the truth regarding their movements on the night in question.
>
> It is my considered opinion that Truman and Utah Wilson are not entitled to clemency or a further stay, and that the judgment entered pursuant to the jury's verdict should now be permitted to take effect.[7]

Hours later, Truman and Utah walked up the stairs to the gallows and were put to death. They each left behind a note. Utah's letter read in part:

To the public; January 2, 1953.

Throughout this whole ordeal Truman and I have told the truth. There has been the inference given many times that in order to save my brother, Truman, I offered him an alibi. This is definitely not so. Neither of us had a thing to do with the Jo Ann Dewey abduction nor her murder.

We thank all the kind people who have and do believe in us. We are thankful too for a wonderful God who has been by our sides constantly.[8]

Truman's letter read in part:

To the public: January 2, 1953.

Utah and I feel that we and our lawyers have done all within the reaches of righteousness to show our innocence. We have told the truth even though the jury wasn't allowed to receive all our case ... So we are leaving our trust in God, and we feel that if we do die for this crime, that someday the facts will be uncovered and show our innocence, even though we may be dead.[9]

The Wilson brothers were not the only ones writing in the hours before the execution. Thomas E. Thomas, age forty-three, of Seattle was arrested for impersonating a federal officer. Thomas, who worked as a furniture salesperson, allegedly sent a telegram fraudulently signed by U.S. Senator Warren G. Magnuson of Washington state, saying a stay of execution had been granted. The telegram reached the Walla Walla prison four minutes after the brothers were put to death. Officials with Western Union told special agents with the F.B.I. that the wording for the telegram was called in from a payphone. Thomas was convicted by a jury for impersonating a federal officer. The Ninth Circuit Court of Appeals later overturned his conviction based on a technicality. A second jury found him guilty and he was sentenced to nine months at a federal work camp on McNeil Island.

A funeral service was held for Truman and Utah at the Little Church of God in Fern Prairie, Washington. The church held sixty people and an overflow crowd listened to the service outside over loudspeakers as rain pelted down. After the open casket ceremony, the Wilson brothers were buried at the Camas cemetery.

Washington State Patrol Cold Case Team

CASE: Hit and Run – Death

VICTIM: Jennifer Bedingfield

Case Synopsis: On Saturday May 8, 1999, two days before Mother's Day, Jennifer Bedingfield and her father were crossing SR 515 (the Benson) at SE 224th St when Jennifer was struck and killed by a vehicle. The vehicle that struck Jennifer fled the scene. Evidence located at the scene indicated the running vehicle was a 1980-1982 blue Datsun 310 passenger vehicle.

Date of incident: May 8, 1999 @ 9:20 PM

Location: SR515 (the Benson) at SE 224th St, Kent Washington

Suspect: 1980-1982 Datsun 310 (similar type vehicle pictured below)

Attention:

If you have information regarding this case please contact the Washington State Patrol Cold Case Team at 425-401-7740 or Stacy.Moate@wsp.wa.gov; reference Case #99-004221. Crime Stoppers is offering a $1,000 reward for information leading to an arrest and charges in this case, see below flyer.

Washington State Patrol Cold Case Team

OF PUGET SOUND

Crime Stoppers of Puget Sound will pay you $1000.00 cash for any information that leads to the arrest and charge of the suspect responsible for the HIT & RUN DEATH of JENNIFER BEDINGFIELD.

Washington State Patrol Detectives are actively investigating a car bicyclist hit and run collision which occurred on Saturday, May 8th, 1999. The incident happened around 9:20 pm in the Kent area on State Route 515 at SE 224th St. The victim, 14 year-old Jennifer Bedingfield, was crossing State Route 515 on her bicycle when she was struck by an unknown driver who fled the area in what was described at the time as a blue or dark brown 1980-82 Datsun 310. The victim Jennifer Bedingfield was critically injured and died a short time later as a result of her injuries. The driver and vehicle fled the scene. The suspect vehicle was later located abandoned in Enumclaw. Washington State Patrol Detectives are asking your help in identifying the suspect driver in the case.

If you have any information about this crime, please call the CRIME STOPPER HOTLINE
@1-800-222-TIPS

VICTIM PHOTO
JENNIFER BEDINGFIELD

Washington State Patrol
Case # 1999-004221

ALL CALLS ARE CONFIDENTIAL AND ALL CALLERS REMAIN ANONYMOUS
IF YOU HAVE ANY INFORMATION CALL
1.800.222.TIPS
SEND A WEB TIP VIA WWW.P3TIPS.COM
DOWNLOAD the MOBILE APP to submit tips VIA a Smart Phone

Washington State Patrol Cold Case Team

Case: 99-005635

Victim: Brian Eugene Helmuth

Case Synopsis:

On June 14, 1999 Alaska State Patrol took a missing person report on Brian Helmuth after he walked away from his family and his job. Alaska State Patrol was able to determine that Brian boarded a plane and landed at the Seatac airport. On June 15, 1999 Washington State Patrol detectives took a missing person report for a man matching Brian's description who went missing off the foot ferry between Bremerton and Seattle. It is believed Brian Helmuth is the same man who went missing off the ferry. No further sightings or trail of Brian's whereabouts have surfaced.

Date of incident: June 14-15, 1999

Location: Missing from Alaska and then missing from Seattle

Suspect: NA

Attention: If you have information regarding this case, please contact the Washington State Patrol Cold Case Team at 425-401-7740 or Stacy.Moate@wsp.wa.gov; reference Case #99-005635.

Washington State Patrol Cold Case Team

Hit and Run - Death

Victim: James Dinh – 3 years old

Case Synopsis: On November 1, 1998 James Dinh was a passenger is his family's vehicle traveling northbound on Interstate 5 approaching 272nd St. A second vehicle lost control when it swerved to avoid striking a vehicle that pulled into lane one from the shoulder. The second vehicle struck the Dinh family's car causing it to go off the roadway, roll in the median and come to rest on its roof in the southbound lanes. A greyhound bus was unable to stop and struck the Dinh's vehicle causing James Dinh to be ejected. James Dinh died shortly after being ejected. Witnesses described the causing vehicle as a white Volvo Station Wagon, similar to the one pictured below.

Date of incident: November 1, 1998 @ 4:45 PM

Location: Northbound Interstate 5 just south of 272nd St, Kent, Washington

Suspect: Heavy set older male with glasses. White Volvo Station Wagon with green and white Washington license plate.

Washington State Patrol Cold Case Team

Similar type vehicle and similar style license plate. Running vehicle described as White Volvo Station Wagon with white and green Washington license plate.

Attention:

If you have information regarding this case please contact the Washington State Patrol Cold Case Team at 425-401-7740 or Stacy.Moate@wsp.wa.gov; reference Case #98-012573.

Washington State Patrol Cold Case Team

Case: Hit and Run - Death

Victim: Edward Reece

Case Synopsis:

On November 23, 1998 at 5:30 PM a vehicle was traveling W/B on SR 900 near S. 129th St. It was dark and raining and the driver did not observed the pedestrain in the roadway and when he changed lanes to the left. When he made his lane change he struck Edward Reece who was crossing the roadway.   As the driver and a separate pedestrian were going to assist Edward a second vehicle drove through the scene striking and killing Edward Reece. The vehicle fled the scene.

Date of incident: November 23, 1998

Location: SR900 near S. 129th St, Renton, Washington

Suspect: Running vehicle described both as dark colored older 'boxier' Honda Accord type hatchback with 'pop-up' head lights and as a beige, tan, or cream colored Mazda 323, 626,or Toyota.

Attention: If you have information regarding this case, please contact the Washington State Patrol Cold Case Team at 425-401-7740 or Stacy.Moate@wsp.wa.gov; reference Case #98-013411.

Washington State Patrol Cold Case Team

Case: Hit and Run - Death

Victim: Peter Schryver

WANTED
FOR
HIT AND RUN

The Washington State Patrol is asking your help locating a brown or olive-colored late 70's or early 80's Jeep CJ. It was last seen leaving the scene of a car/motorcycle hit and run collision on SR-509 near Dash Point State Park on the afternoon of September 1, 1990. One person died as a result of the collision. The Jeep was described as having fog lights on the top, and may have damage on the front. The driver was a white male 25 to 35 years old, 5-10, 160 to 180 pounds, with sandy blond thinning hair and a mustache. The above picture is a composite drawing of the possible driver.

Case Synopsis:

On Septmeber 1, 1990 Peter Schryver was traveling on SR 509 near 4th Ave S in Federal Way when he lost control of his motorcycle in a curve and crashed. Schyver was then struck by a vehicle which caused life ending injuries. The vehicle momentarily stopped and then fled the scene. Witnesses described the running vehicle as a brown late 70's Jeep.

Date of incident: September 1, 1990

Location: SR 509 near 4th Ave S, Federal Way, Washington

Suspect: 70's - 80's brown or olive Jeep CJ. Described as having fog lights on top.

Attention: If you have information regarding this case, please contact the Washington State Patrol Cold Case Team at 425-401-7740 or Stacy.Moate@wsp.wa.gov; reference Case #90-020601992.

 Washington State Patrol
Service With Humility

Washington State Patrol Cold Case Team

Case: Hit and Run - Death

Victim: Judy Tilden

Case Synopsis:

On January 22, 1995 at 2:30 AM a one motorcycle collision occurred NB I-405 at NE 85th St. A passing motorist, Judy Tilden, stopped to provide aid to the injured motorcyclist. While providing aid a vehicle drove through the collision scene striking Judy and the motorcyclist. Judy died as a result of her injuries. The vehicle fled the scene and has not been identified.

Date of incident: January 22, 1995

Location: NB I-405 at NE 85th St

Suspect: A large tan or white Ford car possibly with a partial Washington license plate of 721. Vehicle will have front end damage.

Attention: If you have information regarding this case, please contact the Washington State Patrol Cold Case Team at 425-401-7740 or Stacy.Moate@wsp.wa.gov; reference Case #95-001234.

Washington State Patrol Cold Case Team

Case: Homicide

Victim: Toni Ann Tedder

Toni Tedder

Case Synopsis:

On July 28, 1990, at approximately 5:00 am 18 year old Toni Ann Tedder was killed while she slept on the couch in her family home. Toni Ann's little sister was sleeping on the floor near Toni Ann and woke up to a struggle between her sister and an unknown male intruder. The intruder fled through an open window after being startled by the younger sister. Toni Ann's killer has never been identified.

Date of incident:	July 28, 1990 at approximately 5:00 am
Location:	Clarkston, Washington
Suspect:	Unknown - described as a white male with dark hair
Attention:	If you have information regarding this case, please contact the Washington State Patrol Cold Case Team at 425-401-7740 or Stacy.Moate@wsp.wa.gov; reference Case #WSP90-000001 or call the Clarkston Police Department.

Washington State Patrol Cold Case Team

CASE: Unidentified Remains

VICTIM: Helen Doe

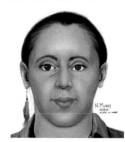

Case Synopsis: On May 14, 1991, a two semi truck collision occurred on southbound Interstate 5 just north of Kalama Washington. The collision resulted in a severe fire killing both occupants of one of the semi-trucks. The driver was identified as Lester Harvel of New Haven Michigan but his female passenger, who was severely burned has never been identified. In 2014 the unidentified females remains were exhumed, a DNA sample was obtained and a forensic sketch was completed based on the skull and witness descriptions. Fuel records indicate Lester Harvel traveled from Missouri through Colorado, Wyoming, Idaho, and Oregon before dropping his load in Washington. It is unknown when or where Lester picked up the female passenger. Below is a map of the route taken by Lester.

VICTIM: Helen Doe, Unidentified female of Native American decent. Approximately 5'1" – 5'4" tall with brown hair and a slight gap between the lower middle teeth. Witnesses stated the female was of a slender build between 110-130 pounds with high cheek bones and a dark complexion. She was last seen wearing Levis, grey shirt, and a black cowboy vest with feather earrings. Autopsy indicated the female had severe scoliosis with a convexity to the right. DNA, dental records, and x-rays are available. Additional info: OCA/MA-91-2120 NamUs case# UP#10449.

Washington State Patrol Cold Case Team

ID Location	City	State	Date	Time
	Fuel Stops			
A	Villa Ridge	Missouri	05/07/1991	17:33
B	xxxxrdia (?) Possibly "Concordia"	Missouri	05/08/1991	15:14
C	Limon	Colorado	05/09/1991	22:43
D	Rock Springs	Wyoming	05/10/1991	12:34
E	Boise	Idaho	05/10/1991	22:25
F	Baker City	Oregon	05/12/1991	12:39
G	Tacoma (drop load)	Washington	05/14/1991	Unk
H	Kalama (crash location)	Washington	05/14/1991	14:45

Attention: If you have information regarding this case please contact the Washington State Patrol Cold Case Team at 425-401-7740 or Stacy.Moate@wsp.wa.gov; reference Case #00-004956

Office of the Chief
Chief John R. Batiste
www.wsp.wa.gov

Captain Neil Weaver
Government and Media Relations

For Immediate Release

January 25, 2022

Sergeant Darren Wright
360-239-0619
Darren.wright@wsp.wa.gov
Twitter: @WaStatePatrol

New sketch for an old case

Kalama WA – Washington State Patrol (WSP) detectives have been working over 30 years to identify the victim of a collision. In May of 1991, an unknown female passenger was riding in a tractor-trailer collision, which ultimately ended in a severe fire. The driver and passenger both perished in the fire. The passenger has yet to be identified, but has been referred to by investigators as Helen Doe.

WSP Detectives, with the help of the group Lost and Missing in Indian Country and forensic artist Natalie Murry, created an updated sketch using current techniques and skills, in a continued effort to bring closure to the family of Helen Doe.

Helen Doe, the unidentified female was of Native American decent. She was approximately 5'1" – 5'4" tall with brown hair and a slight gap between the lower middle teeth. Witnesses stated she was of a slender build between 110-130 pounds with high cheek bones and a dark complexion. She was last seen wearing Levis, grey shirt, and a black cowboy vest with feather earrings. The autopsy indicated Helen Doe had severe scoliosis with a convexity to the right. DNA, dental records, and x-rays are available.

Below left is the original sketch and the updated sketch is on the right.

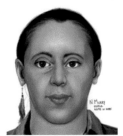 

Above: Washington
State Patrol from 1922.
(*Courtesy Washington
State Patrol*)

Right: Washington
State Patrolman Carder
pictured in 1929.
(*Courtesy Washington
State Patrol*)

Above and below: Washington State Patrol motorcycle troopers. (*Courtesy Washington State Patrol*)

WASHINGTON STATE PATROL
November 14-17, 1933.

CONFERENCE
Washington.

Washington State Patrol, July 1928. (*Courtesy Washington State Patrol*)

An early day vehicle also used as a "paddy wagon." (*Courtesy Washington State Patrol*)

Above left: Washington State Patrol at work behind the scenes. (*Courtesy Washington State Patrol*)

Above right: Washington State Patrol giving a safety presentation. (*Courtesy Washington State Patrol*)

Below: Washington State Patrol's 1978 Plymouth patrol car. (*Courtesy Washington State Patrol*)

Washington State Patrol car with a light bar on top. (*Courtesy Washington State Patrol*)

Washington State Patrol with an early laptop computer. (*Courtesy Washington State Patrol*)

Washington State Police. (*Courtesy Washington State Patrol*)

Washington State Patrol's 1997 Ford Expedition. (*Courtesy Washington State Patrol*)

A group shot of the Washington State Patrol. (*Courtesy Washington State Patrol*)

Washington State Patrol's Ford Crown Victoria from approximately 2010. (*Courtesy Washington State Patrol*)

An addition of SUVs to the fleet. (*Courtesy Washington State Patrol*)

To honor and serve. (*Courtesy Washington State Patrol*)

Washington State Patrol's Ford SUV on patrol. (*Courtesy Washington State Patrol*)

Washington State Patrol's crime laboratory. (*Courtesy Washington State Patrol*)

10

SERGEANT JOHN S. DONLAN

John Donlan was enjoying a Sunday afternoon reading a newspaper in his living room when he heard a noise coming from his basement. He got up from his chair and headed for his hall closet where he kept a loaded gun. Before John could reach the closet, he saw a prowler coming at him. The prowler had entered the hallway after walking up the basement stairs into the house. A violent struggle ensued and the prowler fired his weapon three times. The first shot hit the fireplace mantel. The next two shots hit John. One bullet broke his arm above the elbow. The .32-caliber bullet that hit John underneath his heart, proved to be fatal. John died on the floor of his hallway. His wife, Catherine, and their daughter, Lillian, age twenty-six, found John face down on the floor of the hallway when they returned home late that night. John's loaded firearm was untouched in the hall closet.

When the police arrived just before midnight on May 20, 1934, they discovered the Donlan's basement window of their two-story brick house had been jimmied open. The Donlan's neighbor's house had been entered the same way, but no one was at home next door and nothing was stolen. Another neighboring house showed signs of an attempted burglary, but had not been entered. At the Donlan's house, nothing had been stolen or damaged and the house had not been ransacked.

John, age sixty-four, had been with the Seattle Police Department for thirty-one years. He was a sergeant and had spent the previous two years with the Ballard precinct. All neighboring law enforcement agencies were called upon to assist. Luke May, chief of detectives with the Seattle Police Department, was put in charge of the investigation. He told the media:

> The deadliest type of burglar, is the Sunday afternoon burglar, who doesn't hesitate to invade homes in daylight. He usually figures that

people are away. The Donlan's automobile was gone. There is a high hedge about the place, which shielded him from view. It's a funny situation when even a police sergeant isn't safe in his own home on a quiet Sunday.[1]

Dr. Corson performed the autopsy. He was able to determine John had been shot during the afternoon based on the rigor mortis that had set in. Also, the lights had not been turned on in the house at dusk.

During the previous forty-eight hours, the Seattle Police Department had responded to eighty-one crimes of burglaries, robberies, and larcenies. The burglaries ranged from $20 at one house, $5 at another, and $3 and a strawberry shortcake at yet another house. One burglar made himself a cocktail before ransacking a house. Another burglar stole $50 of jewelry. Two armed men held up a citizen at a downtown intersection and demanded his gold watch and money, which only amounted to some change. A small restaurant was held up at gunpoint by a masked man demanding all of the money from the cash register. The manager of the restaurant handed over $300 and proceeded to run after the suspect but lost him in the crowds on Pike Street.

John was survived by his wife and daughter along with two sisters and five brothers. A service was held at St. James Cathedral with hundreds of people paying their respects. John was laid to rest at Calvary Cemetery. Honorary pallbearers included; Police Chief L. L. Norton, Captains George Comstock, J. J. Haag, and R. W. Olmstead, and Lieutenants L. J. Forbes and D. J. Drew. The active pallbearers were Sergeant W. Dench and Officers Con Walsh, Dan Twohig, E. M. Enochs, P. P. McNamee, and A. F. Evans. Captain Charles Dolphin was put in charge of the police escort from the church to the cemetery.

The police began looking for anyone that John may have arrested that held a grudge against him. They believed the neighbor's burglary may have been a ruse to make it look like a random burglary. The police told the media they had "important clues" but would not elaborate for fear of impeding the investigation.

As the investigation got underway, Detective May located fingerprints on the French doors in the living room of the Donlan home. He also noticed footprints in the dirt outside of the house. Of the three shots fired inside the house, there was only one shell located, which was underneath John's body. John's brother, a retired Seattle police officer, offered a $5,000 reward for the conviction of the person(s) responsible.

Four months after John was murdered in his own home, a man by the name of Edward Griffis, age twenty-one, was captured by the Los Angeles police while burglarizing a house in their jurisdiction. Los Angeles Police

Chief James Davis contacted the police in Seattle after Edward confessed to more than 100 robberies and burglaries, including some in the Seattle area.

Seattle Police Captain of Detectives and the head of the homicide division, Ernest Yoris airmailed all available information on the Donlan case to the Los Angeles Police Department in the hopes they would release Edward to the police in Seattle. Edward had a .32-caliber weapon when he was arrested. The police in Los Angeles located a .38-caliber firearm when they searched his room. Captain Yoris told the media, "We will try and bring him here, but in the event we can't, I will send a man down there to question him."

The following day, Captain Yoris and Detective Lieutenant M. C. Pease began a road trip to Los Angeles to interview their suspect. Detective Lieutenant F. G. Sands told reporters Edward had been on their radar as a possible suspect. They had located a room he rented with his brother in Seattle. They learned the duo moved to Everett, but from there, they lost track of the two brothers.

Lieutenant Sands interviewed Mrs. Angie, who rented a room to Edward while he was in Seattle. She recalled on the day John was murdered, Edward left his room at 11:00 a.m. and returned that evening about 7:30 p.m. She told Lieutenant Sands, "Before he left for Everett, he deliberately put a stolen watch in his little brother's suitcase." The watch was left behind and seized by Lieutenant Sands.

Lieutenant Sands also spoke to Edward's father. He readily admitted his son was "bad," adding that Edward had been stealing since he was in elementary school. Just as quickly, he said he "just knew the boy couldn't be a murderer." When asked, how he knew that, he declined to elaborate. He placed the blame on an unnamed female for educating his son in his criminal endeavors. He also blamed Edward for his own criminal record but would not give further details.

Captain Yoris and Lieutenant Pease met with Edward at the Los Angeles Police Department. After his initial confession, he remained committed to his innocence whenever he was asked. Once confronted by Captain Yoris and Lieutenant Pease with a photograph of Sergeant Donlan, Edward confessed:

> All right, I'll tell you everything I know. I prowled one place first and got money out of a baby's bank. Then I went through a screen window in Donlan's place. He came at me in the hall and asked me what I was doing. I told him I had a gun. He said, "I will take it away from you." And then everything happened so fast—I shot two or three times and I know I hit him once.[2]

Edward admitted he went to a movie theater immediately after the murder. He described the first time he saw news coverage from the local newspaper about the homicide:

> I got scared then, and went to Everett for a couple of weeks. Later, I returned to Seattle for a day or two and then went to Portland from there and I went to Oakland for a while, and then came on to Los Angeles. I figured I had to keep on the move.

He also admitted the murder weapon was one he stole in a previous burglary. By the end of the interview, Edward confessed to nearly 100 burglaries. He told the police he was ready to "face the music."

Deputy Prosecutor Emmett Lenihan sent a telegram to Los Angeles announcing he secured an arrest warrant for first-degree murder clearing the way for Captain Yoris and Lieutenant Pease to return Edward to Washington. Once the Los Angeles Police Department received the arrest warrant, they released Edward into the custody of Captain Yoris and Lieutenant Pease. They drove back to Washington with their prisoner. Edward's father retained attorneys John Fitzpatrick and M. L. Longfellow.

Once back on Washington soil, the detectives took Edward to the Donlan house, accompanied by reporters. Edward showed the police how he first entered the house next to the Donlan's, then walked across the yard, and entered the Donlan's house by forcing the side window of the basement open.

Once inside the house, Edward led them step-by-step as to how the murder took place. He recalled how John asked him, "What are you doing here?" He described picking up two empty shell casings before running out the side door. Edward then showed the detectives how he ran through nearby alleyways. Edward answered all questions put to him as either, "Yes sir" or "No sir." After they left the house, Edward showed them where he threw the murder weapon into Lake Union.

The state had Edward examined by two doctors who concluded, "There was no evidence of delusions, hallucinations or illusions, no evidence of paranoiac tendency and no evidence of mental enfeeblement in his case." They believed Edward was aware of why he was in the county jail awaiting a legal trial. The doctors mentioned Edward's memory for both the past and the present was "quite good."

The defense brought in their own doctors who reported, "something was wrong with his mentality and our talk with him further strengthened our convictions." Edward's father, Peter Griffis, also believed Edward was not capable of standing trial saying, "He's out of his head. He's not responsible for anything he says or does."

After all the reports were completed, Edward entered a plea of not guilty and not guilty due to mental irresponsibility. When reporters interviewed Edward at the jail, he lamented, "Whillikers, it seems like I've spent most of my life behind bars. They sent me to Mercer Island training school after my first burglary when I was eight. I was there two and a half years." Edward added, "I never could see any sense in it."[3] When a reporter asked Edward what "sense" his criminal career made, he replied:

Well, it's taken this long for me to realize there is no sense in that either. I wish I had it to do all over again. I know now what it means to have officers watching every move you make, jailers telling you what you can and can't eat, and everything else that goes with crime and jail. I wish I had learned my lesson just a little sooner.[4]

When the reporters asked about the murder he was accused of, Edward stated, "I'm just going to tell what happened and take my medicine." Edward was then asked, "Well, what did happen?" He simply stated, "I don't remember. I was scared to death, and then, well, then I don't remember what did happen."[5] Edward told the reporters he would plead guilty if his attorneys would allow it.

Edward's trial opened in October 1934, five months after John was murdered. Judge J. T. Ronald presided over the trial. Chief Deputy Prosecutor Emmett Lenihan represented the state of Washington. Edward was represented by the two attorneys his father paid for. The panel of jurists consisted of six men and six women.

The defense explained to the jury that Edward spent a large portion of his youth in the criminal justice system. At the age of eight, he was sent to a training school on Mercer Island after he got into trouble. From there, he was sent to another training school at Chehalis. Once released, he was free for a short period of time before being sent to the Washington State Reformatory at Monroe. When Edward finished his stint at the reformatory, he headed to California. After a short period of time, he returned to Washington state.

Minutes before taking the witness stand, Catherine was heard telling her daughter, Lillian, "It wouldn't bring back John to hang this boy." She quickly added, "Of course, he should be put out of the way behind bars where he can never hurt anyone else as he has hurt us."

Once seated at the witness stand, Catherine broke down sobbing as she described finding her husband on the floor of their hallway. On the witness stand, Catherine became overwhelmed with grief and cried out, "Oh, Johnny, Johnny! Why did you have to leave us that way?" Catherine was unable to complete her testimony and was led from the witness stand.

Edward was seen openly crying, the first emotion that he had displayed up to that time.

Lillian told the jury:

> I unlocked the door and took one step in, and then I tripped over my father's feet. I turned on the light and saw my father lying there. I thought he had fainted, so I began rubbing his hands and kept calling to him, but he never moved.
>
> Mother was hysterical. She was crying. She tried to telephone for help, but the operator couldn't understand her. Finally, I made the operator understand and a police officer came out. About an hour later they told us that father was dead.[6]

Lillian also had to be led from the witness stand after identifying a photograph of her father lying dead on the floor of their home. Catherine and Lillian were excused from the courtroom.

Edward's father, Peter approached Catherine and Lillian outside of the courtroom and was overheard saying:

> I'm so very, very sorry about all this. You can't imagine how terrible this is to me. Eddie has always been a bad boy—ever since he was four years old–but I never thought he would end up this way.
>
> Now everyone is against me. Eddie is against me. He thinks I'm a bad influence on him. And I once went to jail for a crime he committed. His attorneys are against me. They don't like the suggestions I offer at the trial. And I'm the boy's own father. Everyone is against me.[7]

At one point during the trial, Edward lost control momentarily and shouted, "Why all this fuss? I'm ready to plead guilty right now." The trial continued with additional witnesses, one of whom was Captain Yoris who spoke of the police interview he conducted in California wherein Edward confessed to murdering John.

Lieutenant Pease described for the court Edward's demeanor when they visited the crime scene upon returning from California. He informed them that Edward admitted to firing three shots and collecting two of the empty shells before fleeing the crime scene.

Edward's father, Peter, took the witness stand and told the panel of jurists his son was not responsible due to his mental defects. It was his opinion his son had the attitude, "I've only one life to lead—I'm entitled to have my fun without working for it."

Dr. A. W. Hackfield, a psychiatrist from Seattle, agreed with Edward's father, declaring that Edward was indeed insane. Dr. D. A. Nicholson argued that Edward was sane. Edward had his own opinion of the doctors, stating, "I believe they're all nuts."

Edward's maternal grandmother told the jury that days before the trial began, she asked Deputy Prosecutor Lenihan to issue an insanity warrant for Peter, citing that he was not of his right mind. She readily told the jury she believed her deceased husband and two of her daughters; one of whom was Edward's mother, were mentally insane.

As the trial wrapped up, Judge Ronald instructed the jury they needed to return with one of the following verdicts: guilty of first-degree murder with a recommendation of the death penalty; guilty of first-degree murder with life imprisonment; or not guilty by reason of insanity or mental irresponsibility.

The jury chose the second option, thus sparing Edward from the gallows. Two weeks later, Judge Ronald pronounced a sentence of life in prison. In doing so, he told Edward, "Whenever they realize you are ready to become a good man and atone for your act you will be released. I hope you will." In response, Edward simply stated, "I will."

Fourteen years after Edward walked through the doors of the Walla Walla prison, he walked out but he had not been released from custody. He and another inmate escaped by simply walking off the property. Edward's fellow escapee, George Willard Madison, age thirty-eight, was also serving a life sentence for murder. George worked in the photography laboratory. The authorities quickly figured out that before George escaped, he destroyed all photographs of Edward and himself. This caused a delay in releasing photographs of the pair, but nevertheless the authorities were able to get some pictures out to law enforcement agencies and the media.

Four days after the escape, George was captured in Fort Wayne, Indiana. A man noticed a suspicious car in his residential neighborhood and asked two of his neighbors to approach the car with him. George and Edward were asleep in the car when the neighbors looked in. The convicts explained they were lost and were taking a nap. The neighbors asked the men to leave the area. When they failed to do so, the men contacted the police.

Two police officers from the Fort Wayne Police Department arrived on scene. At the request of the police, Edward and George got out of the car. Edward made a run for it, but the police were able to grab George. Edward ran until he reached a 60-foot embankment to a river down below. He plunged down the embankment and swam across the river. The police officer who was not busy holding onto George fired three shots at Edward as he swam, but he managed to get away.

Once at the Fort Wayne police station, George told the officers the two of them had planned the escape. He relayed, "We headed for the Oregon state line. It was really rugged that first night. We advanced only about 15 miles, but it, seemed like we walked about 60." He described how they hid in an orchard before walking to Freewater, Oregon (known today as Milton-Freewater).

George said they tried several cars only to discover they were locked. Then they came across a car with Idaho license plates that was unlocked. They were able to get it started and began driving east. George explained they had $80 in cash when they walked out of the prison. They used those funds for gas and supplies as they traveled. When they reached Chicago, George explained that they tried to get jobs as printers, a skill they learned in prison. When they were unable to produce social security cards, they were turned away.

George said they decided to try and get jobs on a farm. They drove to Fort Wayne and decided to get "a few hours rest" before heading to a farm. They were still resting when the police showed up, according to George.

The Fort Wayne police officers asked George about the clothing and the firearm they found in the stolen car. He explained the clothing and gun were in the car when they stole the vehicle. He added, "A gun always gets you in a bad jam. We just wanted to get away from prison. We thought that if we got far enough from Washington, nobody would find us and we could start life over again." When asked what their reason for escaping was, George blamed it on politics, saying, "I thought my chances for a parole were nil with the new administration."

George told the Fort Wayne officers about his criminal past. He described a robbery at a pharmacy wherein the owner of the business, Henry Anderson, was murdered on December 19, 1930. George described how he and his partners, Michael Deasey, and Martin Casey, went to Henry's drug store to rob him. George was captured two months later. He explained to the police:

We had pulled a few jobs before the Anderson one and went there with no intention of shooting anyone. It was an accident that I shot Anderson and I am sorry that I did it, but I guess I will have to pay.

When I went into the back room and covered Anderson with a gun, he stood up and made a grab for me and I shot. As he fell to the floor, I ran outside with Casey and we got in the car. Deasey threw both of our guns away and we went downtown and abandoned the car at Second and Post after Deasey had gotten out at Second and Division.[8]

George pled guilty to the murder and was sentenced to prison for the remainder of his life. While at Walla Walla prison, he met Edward and they began planning their escape.

Edward managed to avoid capture for six weeks until he was located at a rooming house in New Orleans, Louisiana. He told Detective John Victory that he left Walla Walla prison because he was tired of prison life. He waived extradition and was returned to the Walla Walla prison—for the time being.

The prison doors had barely slammed shut before Edward began planning his next escape. He and another inmate attempted to tunnel their way out of prison. Edward's fellow inmate, Jack Tomlin, age thirty-four, was serving time for a burglary and was due to be released from prison in two years. The two were captured as they attempted to tunnel out underneath the room where the coffins were kept. Prison Superintendent Tom Smith estimated they could have reached freedom in a week to ten days.

Once again, Edward was placed back into a jail cell to begin planning his next escape. In September 1952, he once again made a bid for freedom. He escaped from a minimum-security prison farm.

Three weeks later, Edward was captured in a hotel in downtown Los Angeles. Edward was turned in by a former convict after he asked him for shelter in Los Angeles. Edward told the police in Los Angeles, "I'm a dead duck. When you kill a cop you're through."

II
CATHERINE CLARK

At the end of September 1928, Grover Tyree and F. C. Winklebleck took their wives and children to an abandoned prune orchard to have a picnic and pick some prunes. As they were preparing to leave, Grover's children wanted to get a drink from a nearby stream. As Grover and his children made their way down a ravine, Grover spotted a female body through the dense brush. From a glance, it was apparent that she was no longer alive.

They piled into the Tyree's car and drove several miles to the nearest town and used a telephone to call the authorities. Sheriff Floyd Brower sent Chief Deputy Glenn McEwen and Deputy Hadley to meet up with the men who led them to the body. It was dark by the time they arrived at the ravine. The county prosecutor and coroner followed them to the crime scene. The men used flashlights to see the body. The deputies located a hatchet near the body. Grover immediately recognized the hatchet as one he owned.

The following day, the victim was identified as Catherine Clark, age thirty-six. The investigation revealed she had just arrived in Washington having traveled from her home town of Boston, Massachusetts. The investigators spoke to Grover at length about the hatchet. Grover explained he kept the hatchet in the trunk of his car. He told the detectives he loaned his car to a friend, Archie Moock, who was supposed to return the car the same day, but kept the vehicle overnight. Grover explained the car had just been returned the morning he took his family on the picnic.

Archie was taken into custody. He admitted he borrowed Grover's car to drive Catherine to Idaho so she could meet the man, James Murphy, who she had been corresponding with. The investigation revealed Catherine had been corresponding with a man through a matrimonial bureau. The man she had been exchanging letters with invited her to visit him in Washington with the intent they would marry once she arrived in the Evergreen State.

The deputies located Catherine's luggage at the house Archie shared with his wife and five young children. Buried in Archie's yard was a hatbox, with the letters between Catherine and the man she expected to marry. Also, buried in the yard, wrapped in newspaper was $1,390. Near the Moock's home, a child found an empty purse that the deputies were able to tie to Catherine.

Archie retained the services of attorney, Francis Cavers. Francis told the press, "James Murphy is not a mythical character, but [a] real live man, who we hope to produce as a witness at the trial of Moock." He went on to explain that Catherine's purse was "planted" near Archie's house by an unknown person.

Archie's wife, Tena, adamantly defended her husband, telling the media, "Why, I'd stake my life on his innocence. He couldn't do such a thing. He couldn't even think of it. I've known him since we were children together on farms in Saskatchewan, Canada. He has always been kind." She said Archie was paid $3.60 per day as a millhand. Tena lamented how she was going to support their five children while her husband was in jail. She sent word to her parents in Canada who offered assistance.

Ronald Lindell, who lived near where Catherine's body was located, told the authorities he saw the headlights of a Dodge coupe flash in his window the night before the body was discovered. He described the car as going very fast.

When confronted with one of the letters, Archie told the deputies, the letter was given to him by a messenger when he was downtown. The writer of the letter, purported to be James Murphy, asked Catherine to bring $2,000 to Washington. The writer of the letter promised to reimburse her when she arrived in Washington. The writer explained he was due to inherit a large sum of money if he was married by September 24.

Archie entered a plea of not guilty to first-degree murder. His parents travelled from Canada and stayed for a week before returning home. On December 5, 1928, Archie's trial got underway in Superior Court Judge Huneke's courtroom. Representing the state of Washington were Prosecutor C. W. Greenough and Deputy Prosecutor Louis Bunge. Archie was represented by defense attorneys John Gleason and John Aiken. Seventy-five citizens were called for jury duty. By the end of *voir dire*, four women and eight men, along with two alternates, had been selected.

Grover took the witness stand and explained how he and his family went with the Winklebleck family to pick prunes and enjoy a Sunday afternoon picnic at an abandoned prune orchard. Grover described locating Catherine's body. He told the jury he lent his car to Archie and the hatchet was kept in the car. Grover identified the hatchet that was introduced into evidence, as the one he kept in his car. Grover told the jury:

> My wife, our child and I and Mr. and Mrs. Moock, the Sunday before the body was found, went to the farm. There is an abandoned orchard there and we went to pick fruit. On our return we drove the Moocks home and at their house Moock, as they got out, asked if he could borrow my car for a couple of hours some night during the week and I said he could.
>
> The next Saturday, the day before finding the body, Moock's little girl, Diana, came to my house with a note from him asking if he could borrow the car that evening and I told her yes. He came for it and said he wouldn't be gone long, but he didn't return it until the next morning. He said Moock's only explanation was that he was a little bit late....
>
> Moock had given me $5 to pay for gas and oil he used on the trip and I noticed he had only driven the car by the speedometer about 50 miles. At breakfast I discussed this with my wife and we decided he had paid us too much, so we drove to his home and gave him back $2.50. We said we were going back to the orchard to pick some more fruit and Moock then asked me if he couldn't borrow my car again. I told him that I had promised to go there with the Winkleblecks. 'Wouldn't you take $1 for your bargain and lend me the car?' he asked and I said no.
>
> We drove out there with the Winkleblecks in their car, and we in our car and picked our fruit. Two of the children got thirsty and I took a canteen and started down with them and Winklebleck into the gully, thinking we might find water. One of the little boys caught his toe in the fence and fell down and cried and Winklebleck stopped with him and I went on alone and came onto the body.[1]

Grover explained the body was partially concealed in the brush. He told the jury how he drove into town to summon the authorities. Grover spoke of finding the hatchet near the body and the unique characteristics on the tool that made him know immediately it belonged to him. He told how he and the deputies searched his car later that night and he realized his hatchet was no longer in his car or anywhere on his property.

W. C. Winklebleck corroborated Grover's testimony for the jury. He said he advised Grover to not touch anything at the crime scene and they left the crime scene in order to call the sheriff. He too, identified the hatchet as the one Grover paid 25 cents for. Under cross-examination, defense attorney Gleason demonstrated for the jury that the witness could not remember many recent events, yet he could recall this event in such vivid detail, which he found suspicious.

The prosecution emphasized that once Archie learned the Tyrees were making another trip to the orchard, he requested to borrow their car, in an effort to prevent them from finding the body.

The jury was allowed to view a piece of Catherine's skull along with pieces of her blood-soaked clothing. The prosecution also introduced into evidence the blood-stained grass and soil from where her body lay.

Although photographs were shown to Coroner Collins in an effort for him to identify the victim, the jury was shielded from the photographs due to the graphic nature. Coroner Collins explained Catherine died from a skull fracture and a wound that penetrated two inches through her skull into her brain. The coroner also described wounds from the murder weapon underneath her right eye, and on the back of her head. He added that two of Catherine's front teeth had been broken off during the attack. Upon questioning, Coroner Collins said the blood stains underneath the body indicated she died at that location as opposed to having being killed elsewhere and dumped in the brush.

The day Archie took the witness stand, the courthouse was overflowing with people hoping to get a seat in the courtroom. Archie outlined his background starting at birth on a farm near Yorkton, Saskatchewan, Canada. He spoke of marrying and eventually moving to the United States. Archie told how he met James:

I met James Murphy in the fall of 1926 at the Hedlund box factory, where I was a saw tail-ender. He told me he was working in another part of the mill but I don't know myself where that was. I didn't see him at work, but met him at noon when we were playing ball during the noon hour.

Murphy told me that he wanted to get married through a matrimonial bureau, but didn't want to write himself because he was afraid of a breach of promise case. This was in October or November. I wrote to a matrimonial bureau for a catalog, in January or February, I forget which, in 1928. It was the Floyd Matrimonial agency. I wrote for the catalog under my own name. When I got the catalog I gave it to Murphy. He picked out a woman to write to, and I copied his letter to her.[2]

When asked who the woman was, Archie replied that it was Catherine Clark of Boston. Archie admitted he did not want his wife to find out he was copying James' letters and sending them to Catherine.

It was Archie's testimony that James had been injured in an automobile accident in Idaho days prior to Catherine arriving in Washington. Archie told the court he received a letter via messenger asking him to drive Catherine to the home of James' sister, who resided close to the Spokane bridge. When he was unable to locate the house, he turned the car around and headed back towards the road. It was at that time he came across a car with James and another man in it. Archie said the men gave him a beer but after drinking part of the beer, he fell asleep. It was his belief that he was drugged. He told the jury when he woke up the next morning, the hatchet was missing from the car.

The prosecution showed Archie an enlarged photograph of Catherine's battered body and asked him about the wounds. Archie's defense team immediately objected, stating, "This is unfair tactics on the part of the prosecutor. There is nothing material about these questions and the prosecutor is merely doing it in an effort to unnerve the witness." Judge Huneke allowed the questioning to continue. Archie simply stated "no" to each question about the multiple wounds.

When shown the hatchet, Archie calmly stated, "I never saw it before." He denied ever burying currency or any letters in his backyard. He did admit to writing the letters, but quickly added, they were written at James Murphy's request.

All eyes were on Archie's wife as she made her way to the witness stand. Her voice was barely audible but she offered her testimony to keep her husband from receiving the death penalty. She explained when Catherine arrived from Boston, she stayed with them until she could meet James. She recalled on the day Catherine was murdered, the two of them went to a beauty parlor because Catherine wanted to "get herself fixed up." Tena recalled that Catherine showed her a picture frame and told her that was where she kept her money. When Catherine left that evening with Archie to meet up with James, Catherine asked if it bothered her that the two of them would be driving alone to see James. Tena said she assured Catherine, "No, he could go to the end of the earth with another woman and I know that he would remain true."

After the Moocks finished testifying, the jury was taken to the location where Archie said James and another man met him on the road. A motor stage driver took the panel of jurors, two bailiffs and Sheriff Brower to the road where Archie said he was drugged and passed out. Upon their return, the attorneys presented their closing arguments.

Deputy Prosecutor Bunge turned to the jury and asked:

Who is the only one in this case who knows anything about Murphy? Moock. Who was the last seen alive with Mrs. Clark? Moock. Who brought back Mrs. Catherine Clark's hat box after she was last seen alive? Moock.

Who wrote the letters which lured this poor woman to her death? Moock. On whose premises were these letters and the money found?

Moock's. Who knew Mrs. Clark had money? Moock. Who knew she kept her money in the picture frame? Moock. Near whose home was the picture frame found broken in Mrs. Clark's purse? Moock's. Who had the car in which the murder hatchet was last seen before it was found beside the body? Moock.[3]

Deputy Prosecutor Bunge went on to say, "Mark the secrecy impressed upon Mrs. Clark in these letters. Tell no one; bring only a few personal effects along; bring the letters with her; make no announcement to any one there."[4]

Before Deputy Prosecutor Bunge finished his summary, he stressed:

Money! Money! Money! ... Money predominates every missive Moock mailed to Mrs. Clark. His ardor and love grew as the letters continued, but throughout them all money predominates. Note when you read them in your jury room how he reiterates the need for money. The necessity of Mrs. Clark having it on her in cash, not 'cheques,' the Canadian way of spelling checks.[5]

Before Deputy Prosecutor Bunge turned the closing arguments over to the defense, he emphasized, "Moock was in love with one thing, money—the $1700 Mrs. Clark had."

Defense Attorney Aiken reminded the jury:

The prosecutor has asked you to believe two inconsistent things: that Moock had the cunning and foresight to write those Jim Murphy letters, then to turn around and believe he is so stupid that he didn't attempt to hide the instrument with which he is accused of killing the woman.[6]

He then brought up the subject of the letters. He pointed out the deputies never found any letters from Catherine to James. He concluded the reason behind that was because they were in James' possession. He went on to say:

It was a very peculiar circumstance that they should be found buried there. It is reasonable enough that a man who had committed a murder should bury stolen money, but why should Moock bury the letters? He had no use for them. The logical conclusion is that Mrs. Clark herself buried the letters and the money.[7]

Defense attorney Gleason finished the closing arguments by reminding the jury that Archie was a "simple working man." He informed them Tena had resorted to taking in other people's laundry to support their five children while Archie was in custody at the local jail.

Looking directly at the jury, defense attorney Gleason said:

I don't care whether you believe Moock told the truth or not, and that you believe Murphy had him write the letters, but he took this widow to his home, introduced her to his wife as she told you, introduced her to neighbors and others. Do you mean to tell me this man was planning either to defraud or kill her? He had nothing to conceal.[8]

At 9:20 p.m. on December 13, 1928, the only sound in the courtroom was the ticking of the wall clock until the jury filed into the room. The jury's foreman, W. H. Krause, handed the verdict to the bailiff, George Walker. He in turn handed the paper to Judge Huneke. After he read it, he passed it to the court clerk. As the court clerk read the guilty verdict, Archie dropped his head into his hands. Tena began sobbing uncontrollably until she was led from the courtroom. She expected to be celebrating the twelfth anniversary of their engagement that night, not thinking about her husband hanging for the death of Catherine Clark.

Archie's defense team vowed to appeal based on what they believed was an illegal seizure of the items buried in Archie's backyard. Through tears, Tena told the press, "No matter what they do to Archie, I'll always know he was innocent." On Christmas morning, the Moock children received gifts provided by family friends as their father waited his fate in the county jail.

Archie's case was upheld at every turn. Thousands of citizens signed a petition asking that Archie be allowed to serve a life sentence instead of being sent to the gallows. Archie's family in Canada provided an attorney who travelled from Yorkton, Saskatchewan, to Washington state to fight his death sentence. In the end, it was all for naught as the high courts upheld Archie's case.

As the days grew closer to Archie's hanging, he asked Tena to smuggle a lethal amount of poison to him as he waited his fate on death row at the Walla Walla prison. Sheriff Brower told the media, "Moock became desperate during the last few days he was in the county. We watched very closely because we knew he would attempt to take his own life if the opportunity were given him." Sheriff Brower explained he warned Tena to not succumb to Archie's request. "I told her that if Moock took his own life and it could be proved she gave him the poison, she probably would be charged with murder."

The sound of carpenters building the gallows outside of the Walla Walla prison drowned out the thoughts Archie had while reading the goodbye letters written by his children. Meanwhile Tena was pleading his case in Governor Roland Hartley's office. After a brief meeting, the governor declined to go against the Supreme Court.

Tena was allowed to visit her condemned husband one last time. As she emerged from the prison for the last time, she was sobbing uncontrollably and unable to speak to the waiting reporters. A prison chaplain was sent to speak to Archie in his final hours. Archie walked up the seven steps to his death without saying a word. A funeral was held at St. Patrick's Church, with Tena being the only person in attendance. Archie was buried in a catholic cemetery.

Days later, Tena published the following notice in the *Spokane Chronicle*:

> On behalf of myself and family I wish to thank all my friends who have been so kind and loyal and stood by me during the last two years of darkness and trouble, and also those who signed the petition circulated on behalf of my husband, for their kindness and sympathy.

12

VONNIE JOYCE STUTH

On Christmas Eve 1954, a thirty-nine-year-old woman underwent surgery in St. Petersburg, Florida, after being hit in the head with a wrench before managing to escape from her attacker. Ruby Wesley had just gotten off a bus after working as a cashier at a theater and was walking home carrying Christmas presents for her twelve-year-old son, when her attacker attempted to force her into the parked car that he had just gotten out of. Ruby underwent surgery and spent five days in the hospital before being allowed to return home.

The police in St. Petersburg were already searching for their "bus stop marauder." This case was just the latest in a series of attacks of women walking home from bus stops at night. Two nights prior, a man forced a fourteen-year-old girl into his car. She managed to jump out of the car just as he parked in a secluded area but not before he struck her in her neck. The young girl got away and gave a brief description to the authorities.

A barking dog saved women in two separate incidents when the bus stop marauder attacked them just as they left a bus stop and headed home after dark. In each case, the female managed to escape the clutches of her attacker when he was startled by a barking dog.

The victims who got a look at their attacker were only able to describe the man as tall with curly hair. Up to that point, each victim had managed to escape, but Detective Lieutenant Ralph Lee told reporters they were putting all efforts into the case before "he goes any further," adding the woman who was attacked with a wrench "could easily have been fatal."

Exactly one month later Detective Sergeant Earl Newberry and Detective Clifford Frye spotted a man in a car who appeared to be watching women as they walked from a bus stop at 11:30 p.m. The detectives arrested an eighteen-year-old man by the name of Gary Addison Taylor. Inside Gary's car, they located a Stillson wrench.

The night before Gary's arrest, a woman reported being followed as she walked home from a bus stop. No sooner had she reported the incident to the police, when another female called in a similar report. In each case, a man followed them while driving a car slowly as they walked before the man parked and began following them on foot. In one of the cases, the female screamed and ran to a nearby house where the residents called the police. A neighbor was able to get the license plate of the suspect's car. That license plate matched the car that Gary was seated in when the police arrested him.

Gary denied attacking any females but he was picked out of a police lineup by both women who claimed he had followed them the night before. Ruby identified Gary as her attacker when the police had him repeat the words she recalled hearing, "Don't scream and you won't get hurt." Three additional woman picked Gary out of a police lineup. The police reported that a sketch made from one victim's memory bore a "remarkable likeness" to their suspect. As the number of victims concluded that Gary was the man who accosted them, Gary merely said it was "an amazing series of mistaken identity."

Gary lived with his parents and an older brother in a motel in Treasure Island. Up until his arrest, he had never been in trouble with the law. When the police tried to question him about the series of attacks, they reported he "won't talk" and "flies off the handle and argues whenever they attempt to question him." Gary was moved into solitary confinement after a fellow inmate threatened to "take matters into my own hands and settle with this guy for what he did."

Gary told the authorities he served time in the U.S. Navy. When they checked his military record, they learned he had been discharged after eleven months due to migraine headaches.

The bus stop marauder had his day in Clearwater Circuit Court. The jury was informed they were only to consider the charge of assault with the intent to commit murder for the case against Ruby. They were told they would hear from other women who were followed and/or attacked but that was just to show his identity and mode of operation.

Ruby testified that she was within 150 feet of her home when she was attacked as she walked home from the bus stop. She told the jury her husband and twelve-year-old son found her lying in a ditch when she did not arrive home on time. Her doctor, Benjamin Sullivan, took the witness stand and explained Ruby had suffered a 2-inch laceration to her head and a depressed skull fracture. The police described all fifteen attacks that were reported to them.

Gary took the witness stand and emphatically stated he was at home with his family on Christmas Eve. He did admit to driving to St. Petersburg one night and accosting two women after they disembarked from a bus, but insisted he never touched either of them. Under oath, Gary admitted to telling the police soon after they arrested him that he was "looking for two dames." Gary's father and some of his friends testified that Gary was at home with his family on the night Ruby was attacked.

After listening to all of the testimony, the jury of five men and one woman returned a verdict of not guilty of assault with intent to commit murder for the attack on Ruby Wesley. Lieutenant Earl Newberry later told the media he believed Gary may have been responsible for as many as seventeen attacks in his jurisdiction. He blamed Gary's parents for the acquittal saying, "He was well represented by attorneys. His parents repeatedly told me their son could do no wrong."

The bus stop marauder became the "phantom sniper" of Detroit, Michigan. The police in Detroit were becoming increasingly concerned as citizens were reporting someone shooting in residential neighborhoods. It began on December 22, 1956, when a young girl was shot in the back while walking with her friend. The young girl escaped serious injury even though the bullet was dangerously close to her spine. Two months later, Gary was arrested after a three-hour shooting rampage.

The first sign of trouble was on February 7, 1957:

6:17 p.m. Shirley Eland was shot while she was on her uncle's front porch in Bloomfield Hills minutes after she disembarked from a city bus.

6:40 p.m. two females were shot at a bus stop in Royal Oak.

6:45 p.m. a bullet pierced a car window south of Fourteen Mile and Woodward.

7:50 p.m. the police were summoned for a shooting in Southfield Township.

8:10 p.m. a female reported being shot at in Southfield Township.

8:15 p.m. Wanda Wasik was struck by a bullet whizzing through a window in her house in Southfield Township.

9:05 p.m. after a police chase the phantom sniper was taken into custody in Royal Oak.

Royal Oak Police Officers Howard Lester and Joseph Linville gave chase after spotting the sniper turn down an alley. Gary jumped from the car and was walking away when the officers told him he was wanted. Gary in turn asked, "I beg your pardon?"

Once he was at the police station, Gary readily admitted to being the phantom sniper who had terrorized Detroit for two months. "I just had an urge to shoot at women" was the explanation Gary gave to the investigators. He admitted to several other crimes involving beating and robbing women in Detroit. He summed up his crimes by saying, "I am not a safe person to be at large."

Shirley was treated at the hospital for an injury to her shoulder. Wanda described how the shooting occurred saying, "My back was toward the window when he fired. The thick molding caught the bullet, and it only shattered a window." Wanda's husband, Edwin, added, "The bullet would have caught her in the neck or the head. That molding saved her life."

Once the news broke, Gary's neighbors told the investigators, "Why, he has lived here for almost a year now and we have never noticed one bad thing about the boy. He helped his father a lot around the yard and spent time working on that car of his."

Gary, on the other hand, told the police he frequently had an "urge to hurt women." He expanded by saying the urge began in childhood before apologizing to the police. "I'm sorry about all the trouble I caused. I'm very remorseful. But I have periodic spells in which I can't remember. I'm not responsible."

Initially, Gary was charged with wounding Shirley, although three other females were also injured. In all thirteen people were fired upon. Dr. Ivan LaCore was asked to conduct a psychiatric examination on Gary. He concluded that Gary was "dangerously mentally ill and should be hospitalized." Prosecutor Frederick Ziem began the process of requesting a sanity hearing. Gary was deemed to be insane and was committed to the Ionia State Hospital for the criminally insane after three psychiatrists testified that they believed Gary was criminally insane. Referring to Gary, Dr. Clinton Mumby wrote in his report, "will need confinement for the rest of his life in a maximum-security institution." Gary told Circuit Judge Frank Doty, "This is what I have wanted, it is all over now but the crying."

Four years later, the police in Detroit were shocked when they learned Gary had been released from the state hospital without their knowledge. In checking with the officials at the Ionia State Hospital, they learned Gary was supposed to remain there "until his sanity is restored." Two years after Gary entered the facility, the medical superintendent sent a letter to Prosecutor Ziem stating Gary had recovered from his psychosis and "will no longer be a menace to society." When the prosecutor wrote a letter vehemently opposing Gary's release, the superintendent withdrew the release documents, but wrote a letter to Prosecutor Ziem stating in part:

> He has improved to the degree that it is the opinion of the psychiatric staff that he would be able to make a satisfactory adjustment in the open

community without danger to the public welfare and should be granted a visit on a convalescent basis and, eventually a parole.[1]

Gary was examined by a panel of psychiatrists after the exchange of letters. Months later the medical superintendent requested that Gary be allowed to take a convalescent role at the Lafayette Clinic. The officials believed Gary would be in a maximum-security area and would only be at the clinic for a short period of time "for further psychiatric study." As it turned out, Gary was allowed to leave the facility to attend a trade school for welders during the week and live off campus.

The police in Detroit only learned Gary was free, after Addie Dixon, age fifty-three, and her daughter, Barbara Kraus, age thirty, reported being attacked by their tenant. Detectives arrived and learned Addie had rented a room to Gary. Neither of the women were seriously injured. Gary was arrested and admitted he attacked Addie and Barbara with a machete. He was returned to the Ionia State Hospital.

The public was outraged that Gary had been roaming the streets of Detroit without anyone's knowledge. Michigan Governor released the following statement:

A review of the case indicates that at the time there existed reasonable indication that parole to the clinic would aid in the rehabilitation process. What appeared to be a good risk calculated to restore a patient to a responsible and useful role in society developed to be an error in institutional judgment.[2]

In 1966, Gary was released from the Ionia State Hospital but he still faced charges from the sniper attacks in Detroit from 1957. The trial was held without a jury before Oakland County Circuit Judge Arthur Moore. Judge Moore ruled Gary was insane at the time of the sniper attacks. In his ruling, Judge Moore stated:

The good facets of Gary Taylor's community failed him while he was much younger. I hope that the public, through the example of this case, will be less prone to ignore the behavior of youth around them and look favorably upon reporting to public and private agencies the truth within their knowledge.[3]

Once again, Gary was ordered to remain in the Ionia State Hospital.

The following year, Gary was back in court for a habeas corpus hearing requesting that he be released from custody. His request was denied with the adage he would "present a grave danger to members of society" if he was allowed to be a free member of society.

The next time Gary crossed paths with law enforcement was in 1975 in Houston, Texas. He had been released from a mental hospital in Michigan three years before with the condition he check in on a regular basis, which he failed to do. Instead, Gary married a young lady and they moved to Onsted, Michigan. After a short time, they moved to Enumclaw, Washington. They marriage broke up and Gary moved to Houston, Texas.

Once again, Gary was in handcuffs sitting in a police station confessing to harming females. This time he confessed to murdering four women since he walked out of the state hospital as a free man. Gary came to the attention of Texas law enforcement after allegedly raping a sixteen-year-old girl.

Among the women Gary claimed to have killed was Vonnie Joyce Stuth, age nineteen of Enumclaw. Vonnie's disappearance the previous Thanksgiving had led to an extensive search but she was never found. Her disappearance remained unsolved at the time authorities in Texas made the phone call to Washington.

On Thanksgiving Day in 1974, Vonnie's husband contacted law enforcement when he arrived home from work early in the morning and discovered his wife was nowhere to be found. Their front door was unlocked, their television was on, and a partially prepared salad was on the kitchen counter. The investigation revealed Vonnie had last spoken to a relative the night before her disappearance. Detectives questioned a male neighbor of the Stuth's but did not have enough to hold him.

"Exactly where he said it would be," were the words spoken by detectives with the King County Sheriff's Office upon locating Vonnie's body in a shallow grave in the backyard of a house Gary rented in Enumclaw. Vonnie had been shot in the head. The investigation showed Gary lived in Enumclaw for a brief period of time after leaving Michigan. It turned out Gary was the neighbor the detectives questioned after Vonnie disappeared. Gary left Washington state soon after Vonnie disappeared.

Law enforcement unearthed the bodies of Lee Fletcher, age twenty-four, and Debbie Henneman, age seventeen, in Onsted, Michigan. The two females were buried in the backyard of a house where Gary lived at one time. These were two of the females Gary told the authorities in Texas he had murdered. He also confessed to killing Susan Jordan, age twenty-one in Texas. Susan's body was located and turned over to her family for a proper burial.

The authorities in Washington began the extradition process and requested Gary be held without bail on a fugitive warrant. Texas District Court Judge William Hatten ordered Gary be extradited to Washington but Gary's attorneys fought the process. The Texas Court of Appeals sided with the defense stating Gary's attorneys were not given enough time to prepare for his defense.

Eventually, Gary was extradited to Washington where he entered a plea of innocent. A month later, he appeared before King County Superior Court Judge William Goodloe and entered a plea of guilty to second-degree murder. As part of the plea bargain for a lesser charge, it was agreed that Gary would not be tried for the murder of Susan in Texas or the two females in Michigan. Gary told the court he shot Vonnie in the head after she began screaming for help. He then shot her at close range before burying her body in the backyard of the house he was renting. The prosecution agreed to the reduced charge over concern that Gary's confession in Texas would not be admissible in court. Judge Goodloe sentenced Gary to life in prison. In doing so, he said he would recommend that Gary not be paroled after the minimum fifteen years adding that Gary should never walk free again. The Washington State Board of Prison Terms and Paroles recommended a sentence of ninety years in prison.

As of 2023, Gary remains in custody at the Washington State Penitentiary. He is eighty-six years old.

13

NANETTE MARIE MARTIN

Thirteen-year-old Nanette Marie Martin began her day at 3:30 a.m. on Saturday, April 3, 1976, when she picked up a bundle of newspapers in downtown Spokane. She started delivering the newspapers but when she did not return home by 8 a.m., her parents contacted the Spokane Police Department.

Detectives were able to ascertain she picked up approximately 100 newspapers for her route. They learned Nanette had only delivered about one dozen newspapers spread between two apartment complexes and one house. From there, she seemingly vanished into thin air. Uniformed police officers canvassed the area but came up empty handed.

Nanette was in the eighth grade at Havermale Junior High School. She was days away from turning fourteen years old. She had been delivering newspapers since the previous September. Her mother told the reporters her missing daughter enjoyed sewing and cooking and was a quiet child. The night before, she had gone roller skating with her stepfather and her ten-year-old sister. Nanette had plans to go kite flying Saturday afternoon.

The police did not believe Nanette had run away from home, and right from the start, feared she had been abducted while delivering newspapers in the north section of Spokane. Spokane Police Detective Robert Van Leuven told the media:

> She went out to deliver papers and she hasn't been seen since—that's all we know for sure. Sometimes her dad takes her on her route if she has a heavy bundle and sometimes she goes with her sister, but this time she went on her own.

Two days after her disappearance, Detective Robert Bailor located Nanette's body inside a plastic bag in a swampy area on the outskirts of town. Later, Detective Bailor told reporters, "I was just out looking. It's one of those things you hope you don't find. I wanted to find her alive."

The county coroner, Dr. Lois Shanks, determined Nanette had been raped and strangled to death before being placed in plastic bags. She confirmed Nanette's nude body had been dismembered prior to being placed in plastic bags. Dr. Shanks believed Nanette had not been there for long before being discovered. She added, "The place where the girl's body was found was not where she was killed."

Detective Lieutenant Fred Fait told the reporters, "We have no solid leads as to the identity of the killer, but we are following a few leads that we have in the case." Detective Lieutenant Fait said they had added additional officers and detectives to the case as they searched for the murderer. They were also searching for Nanette's clothing, eyeglasses, newspapers, and her newspaper delivery bag. A fund was established for the arrest and conviction of the person(s) responsible for Nanette's murder.

Two weeks passed and despite answering "scores" of telephone tips and following up on hundreds of leads, the police were still baffled as to who committed the murder. The day before Easter Sunday, the mayor of Spokane, David Rodgers, and Spokane Police Chief Wayne Hendren teamed up and wrote the following letter that was published in the *Spokane Chronicle*:

> To the abductor of Nanette Marie Martin:
> We know you are living a life of torment–that your nights are without sleep and your days are spent in terror and misgiving.
> We urge that you now surrender yourself to proper authorities and bring to an end the mental anguish and confusion that have been your constant companions for the past two weeks. You can receive the help you need by giving yourself into custody.
> It is our sincere belief that you are in a very serious emotional state and are in urgent need of psychiatric care. Perhaps you also desire religious counseling that you have been afraid to seek on your own. If you give yourself up, these services will be made available to you.
> It is our pledge that your person and your rights will be fully protected. You will receive absolutely fair treatment at all times, including access to legal counsel.[1]

The letter was signed by Mayor Rodgers and Police Chief Hendren. Their contact information was listed in the newspaper.

A broken window in a rental apartment was the break the police needed. Thomas Mahrt's landlord entered one of the apartments he owned to repair a broken window. Once inside the apartment, he saw what he believed were photographs depicting Nanette's body. He telephoned the police who immediately notified the detective team.

The detectives were granted a search warrant for Thomas' apartment. They located a newspaper delivery bag, with newspapers dated the day Nanette would have been working her delivery route, glasses and clothing, all of which they believed belonged to Nanette. They also found plastic bags similar to the bags that held Nanette's body. The detectives seized the photographs that the landlord found, two vehicles that belonged to Thomas, and the property they believed belonged to Nanette.

Nineteen days after Nanette disappeared, Spokane Police Detectives Charles Staudinger and Robert Van Leuven slapped a pair of handcuffs on Thomas Mahrt, age twenty-eight. Thomas was formally charged with first-degree murder and first-degree kidnapping. He was held without bail in the maximum-security section of the Spokane County jail.

Thomas' first run-in with the law was when he was thirteen years old. He was caught vandalizing and desecrating churches and starting fires. He was sent to the Eastern State Hospital for ninety days. After he was caught committing the same crimes a year later, he spent time in a state-run facility for juveniles.

Upon graduating from high school, Thomas joined the military and spent two years in Germany and eight months in Vietnam. He earned a bronze star and an Air Combat Medal during the 175 hours of combat he served as a helicopter crew chief.

Once back in Washington, he worked as a printer at his family's business. He and his wife were in the process of divorcing prior to his arrest. They had a four-year-old boy.

When the detectives spoke with Thomas, he told them he was driving home from a restaurant early on the morning of April 3 when he spotted what he believed to be a newspaper delivery boy. He decided to stop and purchase a newspaper. When he realized the newspaper delivery person was a young female, he was overcome with ideas of rape. He grabbed the pistol that he kept in his car and forced Nanette to get in his vehicle. He drove her to his apartment where he raped her before strangling her to death with a necktie. He hung her nude body from the stairs in his basement then left the apartment to go to work.

Thomas explained to the investigators that when he returned home from work, he planned to dispose of her body but was unable to due to people attending a party at his neighbor's apartment. Thomas said the following day he went out and purchased a camera. He admitted he took photographs of Nanette's body before using a hunting knife to dismember her body. Thomas told the detectives he placed the body parts in plastic bags and drove to the outskirts of town where he left the plastic bags containing Nanette's body.

A check of Thomas' tires revealed they matched tire tracks near where Nanette's body was recovered. The investigators also found blood in the trunk of Thomas' car. Detectives located the necktie in Thomas' apartment along with a note he allegedly wrote. The note was never finished but it began:

> Nanette Marie Martin, 13 years, life of senseless crime and murder, 3 a.m. 3 April, 1976. I was on my way home from Casey's Restaurant after eating breakfast when I saw a paperboy walking up Mission. He had a scrawny, underfed appearance. It was this that got up my courage because he wouldn't be able to fight back. I drove up the ...[2]

During a court-ordered psychiatric examination, Thomas told the psychiatrist he would "do the same thing again," if he thought he could get away with it. Two psychiatrists examined Thomas and both recommended that he not be allowed to go free. They believed he was competent to stand trial and knew the difference between right and wrong the morning he abducted and murdered Nanette.

"Guilty" was the one-word answer Thomas gave to the question of how he pled to the charges of first-degree murder and first-degree kidnapping. Superior Court Judge George Shields asked Thomas to describe in his own words what he had done. Thomas simply stated, "I kidnaped and killed Nanette Martin." Judge Shields sentenced Thomas to two consecutive life terms in prison. Each term required a minimum of twenty years in prison. Judge Shields explained with good behavior Thomas' sentence could be reduced to less than twenty-nine years unless the parole board waived the mandatory minimums.

In 1990, the Indeterminate Sentence Review Board ordered Thomas to serve 166 years in prison. As of 2023, Thomas remains in custody of the Washington State Department of Corrections. He is seventy-four years old.

14
HAROLD OSTER

November 17, 1959, dawned like any other day in Camas, but by the end of the day, the police were dealing with a homicide, an armed robbery, an auto theft, a double kidnaping, and a shootout at a police roadblock.

"Don't give me any trouble, I just killed a man five minutes ago," repeated Carl Gehman to the police. Carl was describing the man who held him at gunpoint before locking him in the basement of the sporting goods store he owned, Gehman's Sports Center. Carl told Camas Police Captain Jim Bourland and Chief Criminal Deputy Herb Russell of the Clark County Sheriff's Office that a man came into his store the previous Saturday and ordered a .22-caliber revolver. The man returned on Monday and picked up the weapon. He returned on Tuesday and wanted to exchange the revolver for a Browning 9-millimeter automatic pistol.

Carl told the police he explained to the customer he would have to wait the required two days per state law. He said the customer asked to see some ammunition and when Carl returned with the ammunition, the customer was pointing the .22-caliber revolver at him. He ordered Carl into the basement and that was when he told Carl he had just killed a man. Carl told the police the customer left after he locked Carl in the basement. Carl told the police, the man did not appear to be shaken or nervous, but instead, was quite calm. Carl said he was able to crawl through an opening above the door and immediately notify law enforcement.

The police checked the registration card from when the man ordered the .22-caliber four days before. The man used the name John R. Broderson, age thirty-four, and listed an address of a rooming house in Camas that was across the street from the Gehman's Sport Center.

When law enforcement arrived at the boarding house, they located the murder victim, Harold Oster, age fifty-one. His hands and feet were bound with adhesive tape and a gag had been taped inside his mouth. He had been bludgeoned and stabbed multiple times in the back. The police found a 9-inch knife in a closet in the apartment.

County Coroner Paul Mylan worked with Tacoma pathologist Dr. Charles Larson later that evening to determine the cause of death. Their investigation showed Harold had been stabbed five times. Two of the stab wounds passed clear through his body, then into a blanket and a mattress pad. One of the wounds passed through Harold's heart. Harold had been hit with great force on the head three times, one of which caused a severe skull fracture. Coroner Mylan said the injuries occurred after the victim had been bound and gagged.

As the coroner was doing his investigation, the police were searching for John. Through their investigation they learned Harold worked as a salesperson for an automobile company where he had been employed for the past six weeks. The police theorized John asked Harold to bring a car by his apartment in a ruse by saying he was interested in purchasing a car. In checking with the auto dealership, Harold worked for, the police learned a car was missing from their lot. An all-points bulletin was issued for the vehicle. The police pieced together that John had arrived in Camas from Oceanside, California the week before the homicide. He had applied for several jobs but was not working at the time of the murder.

That afternoon, Mr. and Mrs. James Tucker were driving their station wagon on Highway 30 towards the Dalles, Oregon, when they came across a man standing next to a broken-down car. They stopped and gave the man a ride. Mrs. Tucker later told the police that everything was fine in the beginning but then the man's voice became demanding and when she turned to look at him in the backseat, he was pointing a gun at her. He yelled at the couple, "Don't ever pick up a hitchhiker!"

Mrs. Tucker began crying, and the hitchhiker demanded she stop crying. She recalled the man telling them he had just beaten a man to death in Camas and stolen his car, which was the vehicle stalled on the side of the road. Mrs. Tucker recalled the conversation for the detectives saying, "He offered to let me out of the car, and told me he would take Jim with him." She said she immediately told him, "No, no, no, where Jim goes, I go. He promised he would not hurt a hair on my husband's head, and he let me out of the car. We shook hands and he let me out ... right in the middle of the Dalles."[1]

Mrs. Tucker watched as the station wagon drove away and then ran to a nearby business and asked to use the telephone to call the police. She informed them a man had her husband at gunpoint and was forcing him to drive on Highway 30 through the Dalles.

Oregon State Police Officer Kenneth Green heard the description of the vehicle and went in pursuit. He had just caught up to the station wagon, when suddenly the station wagon stopped in the road. John leaped from the station wagon and held Officer Green at gunpoint. He released James but took Officer Green as his hostage. John had both the .22-caliber and the 9-mm weapons trained at Officer Green.

John started to slow down as he approached a police roadblock set up for him near Arlington, Oregon. When the car slowed, Officer Green attempted to push the weapons down that were pointing at him. The two grappled with the weapons. Both weapons went off, with a bullet hitting Officer Green in his thigh and John in his leg. Officer Green managed to hold John down until backup officers could arrive and take him into custody.

Officer Green and John were transported to a hospital in Umatilla, Oregon. Officer Green was then taken to a hospital in the Dalles and John was taken to a hospital in Pendleton. When John was ready to be released, Sheriff Clarence McKay, Camas Police Chief Leonard Wright, and Washington State Patrol Lieutenant Marvin Paulson drove to Pendleton to transport John to the Clark County jail. He was held without bail pending his trial. Judge Eugene Cushing appointed public defenders James Gregg and William Boettcher to represent John.

At first, John pled innocent to the charge of first-degree murder. His attorneys later changed it to a plea of temporary insanity. A week before John's trial was to begin, additional prospective jurors were asked to report for jury duty.

In a strange turn of events, a fellow inmate told the jailor that John planned to take the court stenographer hostage and kill the judge during his next court appearance. John denied ever telling his fellow inmate that he planned any violence towards either the judge or the court stenographer. John also admitted he had had the opportunity to escape after another inmate cut the bars to their community cell. John told his attorney, "I have no desire to be a fugitive or to run around at night. If I had escaped, I would have to go around as a murderer, and I might have to kill again and again."

The trial opened six months after Harold was murdered. Judge Cushing presided over the trial that opened to a packed audience. The state was represented by Clark County Prosecutor Dewitt Jones.

John's defense attorney, William Boettcher, gave the jury some background information on his client. He said John quit school when he was a sophomore in high school. At the age of seventeen, John joined the U.S. Navy. John, he said, served aboard the aircraft carrier *Enterprise* and was involved in three major sea battles during World War II, including one where he was blown off the ship and landed in the ocean.

Boettcher explained that John began having episodes where he would pass out and not remember anything that led to him being discharged. Once he left the military, he suffered from depression. He did rejoin the military during the Korean War. Problems ensued and he was discharged as "mentally unfit." While living in southern California, John attended church, taught bible studies, and sang in the church choir, according to his defense attorney.

Before John took the witness stand, he requested through his attorneys that he be allowed to place his hand on a bible when he was sworn in. Other witnesses simply agreed to tell the truth without using a bible. The judge granted John's request. John told the court he had only been in Camas for a short time. He said he left California and tried to find work in Portland, Oregon, but was unable to. He said he was in the process of divorcing his third wife who lived in California with their seven-year-old son. John said he wanted to get his son and start a new life in another country.

John admitted he had recently held a rifle on his in-laws for an entire day, demanding they tell him where his estranged wife was living with their child. He eventually put the weapon down and accepted their offer of a bus ticket to Portland and $250 in exchange for not contacting any of them in the future.

John immediately told the panel of jurors, "I did not plan the killing. It was an act of impulse." John added that "something just snapped." However, the prosecution introduced a statement John wrote on his first day in jail confessing to planning the murder. When the statement was read in court, John said, "It was not a true statement, but one I wanted to give because I didn't care to go on living."

John explained he rented a room at the boarding house and was trying to find a job in Camas. He said he applied at a paper mill and was waiting to hear back from the company. He stated he went to the used car lot to look for a car to buy. The following day, he went to Gehman's Sport Center and ordered a .22-caliber pistol. When asked by his attorney, why he purchased a gun, John said, "I thought I'd try it the other way for a while."

John explained after he ordered the weapon, he returned to the automobile dealership to take a car for a test drive. He was asked who took him for the test drive and he replied, "This Oster." He went on to say, "I had not been thinking about buying that car because I did not have the funds, or even thinking about taking it."

John testified that evening he watched television with his landlady and her sister before going to his room where he "just sat and thought." The following morning, he said he ate some breakfast then went and purchased a hat and gloves before returning to the automobile dealership. Once at the dealership, he said he made up a story about having an invalid wife back at the boarding house who was the "purse holder." He said he asked Harold to come to his room.

John readily admitted that as soon as Harold arrived, he pulled out his .22-caliber weapon but said it was unloaded. He admitted to binding Harold's feet and hands and telling him, "Lay there and be quiet. Someone will eventually come along to let you go. I only want your car for transportation and I will leave it by a police station or somewhere so you will get it back."

John told the jury he went into the bathroom but when he heard Harold moaning, he went back into the room and said, "Now you be quiet." John described leaving the room and heading down the stairs when he heard Harold "hollering and really groaning." John said, "something just snapped." He recalled going back into the room and grabbing his bolo knife. John admitted he hit Harold on the head two times before proceeding to stab him. He said he threw the knife in the closet and left the boarding house.

After that, John said, he went to Gehman's Sport Center where he held up Carl before leaving with the 9-mm weapon. John said he left Carl locked in the basement and went back to the stolen car, but not before he stopped and asked a Camas police officer about possibly joining the police force's reserve unit.

From there, John said, he drove to the outskirts of town where he loaded both weapons. John remembered driving to Vancouver, before crossing the bridge into Oregon and driving east on Highway 30. He told the jury he kidnapped the Tuckers after they stopped to help him.

John readily admitted he trained the weapons on Officer Green and said he could have killed him at any time. John emphasized to the jury he never killed the Tuckers or Officer Green, even though he had the opportunity to do so. As for Harold, he stressed, "If I'd intended killing that man, I'd never taken him to my room or left behind my identification and clothing. I'd have taken him to a wooded area, stripped his body and buried him in a shallow grave."[2]

The prosecution asked a series of questions regarding whether or not John knew it was wrong to stab Harold and to strike him on the head. John answered both questions in the affirmative. John was asked why he went back to Gehman's Sport Center to get another weapon, referring to the 9-mm. John answered that the .22-caliber he already had would not be sufficient for the "life of crime" he was planning. He then described he wanted to "knock over" the payroll office at the Camp Pendleton Marine base near his former home in California. He estimated he could get away with as much as $300,000.

Prosecuting Attorney Jones described John as "an architect of crime," then added, "it would be difficult for a mind to make up a more sordid train of events." Countering the defense who referred to John as anti-social, the prosecution said, "he is anti-law abiding. He knows the law and he knows when he violates the law. He knows in his own mind that he had violated the laws of God and man."[3]

Defense attorney Boettcher told the jurors that John was probably guilty of unpremeditated second-degree murder, but not first-degree murder:

> The crime is not that of first-degree murder, because the defendant could form no criminal intent or make a rational distinction between right and wrong. We feel he should be confined to the criminally insane ward at the state penitentiary.[4]

The eight men and four women of the jury felt otherwise, returning a verdict of guilty of first-degree murder with a recommendation for the death penalty. Superior Court Judge Cushing sentenced John to hang for the murder of Harold on June 25, 1960, four weeks in the future. John requested the date be moved up and explained he planned to fast until he was put to death, adding that he had not eaten in three days.

"I've made my peace and I'm ready to go. My only wish is that the execution could be sooner," However, once John arrived at the Washington State Penitentiary, he ended his fast and began eating with what the prison officials described as "gusto."

The American Civil Liberties Union filed an appeal with the State Supreme Court, against John's wishes. The State Supreme Court did not overturn the court's decision. Governor Albert Rosellini declined to get involved. Upon arriving at the gallows, John asked, "Where do I stand?" Once that was explained to him, John stated, "I'm ready to die. I hope it doesn't take long." John was hanged at 12:01 a.m. on June 25, 1960.

15
WAH MEE CLUB

Early on the morning of February 18, 1983, the police were asked to check on a man lying against the wall in Maynard Alley. As the police approached the man, he pointed to the door of the Wah Mee Club in Seattle's Chinatown. The police entered the eerily quiet business and discovered the bodies of thirteen people, all of whom had been shot dead. Eleven men and one woman lay dead on the floor of the private club, having been bound and shot execution-style. When the police officers walked into the office area of the business, they discovered the body of a man, although not bound, had also been shot in the head.

One victim was barely alive and rushed to Harborview Medical Center where he succumbed to his injuries. The man who had been lying in the alley was rushed to the hospital and kept under heavy police guard in the hopes he could tell the officers what occurred after he received medical care.

The investigation quickly unfolded as the police learned the Wah Mee Club was a private club. Anyone entering the club had to be admitted through two separate doors, both of which were closely monitored. The patrons had to know the correct password and signal in order to gain entry to the business. Once inside the club, members played card games, drank alcohol, and socialized.

The police surmised more than one killer was responsible for the mass shooting. They described the murders as "very methodical." All but the one victim had been hog-tied and shot one or more times. A total of thirty-two bullets had been fired.

The injured man was identified as sixty-one-year-old Wai Chin. He had been shot in the face and throat but survived. He underwent surgery for the gunshot wound to his neck. Using written notes and nodding his head,

Wai was able to describe for the police what took place inside the private club. He identified two of the shooters; Benjamin Ng, age twenty, and Kwan Mak, age twenty-two. He was not able to identify a third shooter.

Wai explained to the investigators that there were seven or eight people in the club, when Kwan and the third suspect entered the club just before midnight. Benjamin entered a short time later and suddenly the three men held the patrons at gunpoint while they hog-tied them and robbed each person. They permitted additional people into the club, and immediately hog-tied them and robbed them of their money. At one point they began firing using small-caliber handguns. Wai told the detectives that as soon as he was shot, he passed out. When he came to, he managed to untie his hands and feet and stagger outside. Wai credited his survival due to the fact he was able to crawl under a table when the shooting began. When the bullets hit him under the table, they came in at an angle, versus straight on.

The police quickly rounded up both suspects. Benjamin was asleep in his bed when the police arrived armed with a search warrant. In Benjamin's room, they located two loaded .38-caliber revolvers, a semi-automobile rifle, and four loaded clips. The police seized $10,360 from his bedroom and four pairs of surgical gloves.

Kwan turned himself in at the urging of his family. The police seized a loaded .357 revolver, two pistols, two rifles, two shotguns, ammunition, and almost $5,000 in cash. They seized two cars from Kwan's property, one of which had a length of white cord in plain view.

The victims were identified as: Jean Mar (the only female), her husband, Moo Min Mar, Henning Chinn, Wing Wong, Hung Fat Gee, John Loui, Chon L. Chinn, Dewey Mar, Gim Lun Wong, George Mar, Jack Mar, Chin Wing, and Chinn Lee Law.

The police asked the public for assistance in identifying the third suspect. They held a press conference and stated, "We need your help in trying to find out who may have been with those two men in Chinatown, particularly on that evening."

The police came under fire for allowing the vice operation to exist. Seattle Police Major Dean Olson told the press "The club had been closed since the mid-70s, operating sporadically since that time." He said it had recently "quietly opened up." Seattle Police Chief Patrick Fitzsimons told the media that the screening of members and the unwritten code of silence along with secret passwords to enter the private club made it difficult to be aware of what was happening. He denied knowing there was high-stakes gambling taking place in the club.

Benjamin and Kwan both pled innocent to thirteen counts of aggravated first-degree murder and one count of first-degree assault for wounding Wai.

Wai was making progress at the hospital when he suffered a setback two weeks after the shooting. During his surgery, the doctors were not able to remove all of the bullet. The fragments of the bullet created problems. The trauma team at Harborview Medical Center were able to get Wai back on the road to recovery. Three weeks after the shooting, Wai was able to speak. When he was released from the hospital, he was secured in a secret location under twenty-four-hour police guard for his own safety. Seattle Police Major Dale Douglass told reporters, "We don't want anyone to find him. We don't want to take any chances."

The third suspect was identified as Wai-Chiu Ng (no relation to Benjamin). A no-bail international arrest warrant was issued.

Two of Kwan's relatives pled guilty to tampering with evidence. They admitted to cleaning Kwan's vehicle after the shooting, before the police seized the car.

When the court doors swung open six months after the shooting, the third suspect still had not been captured. Seattle Police Major Douglass told the media, "We don't know where he is or we'd arrest him."

King County Superior Court Judge Frank Howard agreed to separate the trials of Benjamin and Kwan, at the request of the defense attorneys. Benjamin's trial was the first one held. Representing the state of Washington were Senior Deputy Prosecutors Robert Lasnik and William Downing. Benjamin was represented by John Henry Browne and David Wohl.

The trial was moved to the courtroom as close as possible to the jail on the top floor where Benjamin was being housed. Deputies explained, "Security measures are being taken in this case due to the nature of the charges and for the protection of the defendant."

Seating a jury proved difficult with more than a hundred prospective jurors being called. Defense Attorney Brown warned the citizens, "I can't overstate how gruesome [the photographs] are going to be. The state will introduce some gruesome photographs and chilling testimony and will paint a picture of a real disaster."

Once the eight men and four women of the jury were seated, the defense team asked the judge to sequester the jury. Judge Howard assured the panel of jurors that unless it became absolutely necessary, he did not intend to "pull you out of your homes during this trial."

In his opening remarks, King County Prosecutor Bill Downing told the court that the trio went into the establishment with the intention of committing a robbery. In order for there to be no witnesses to the crime, they began shooting everyone inside. What they did not count on, Prosecutor Downing explained, was that one person would be able to escape and summon help. He explained this situation was unique compared to other robberies in that in order for the suspects to gain entrance to the business, they had to be recognized by the person working the door security detail. That created a situation where there would be witnesses who could identify them by name.

The prosecution introduced into evidence a paper bill seized from the money in Benjamin's room. Prosecutor Downing told the jury the bill bore the fingerprint of one of the victims.

The defense did not try to deny Benjamin was at the club the night the shooting took place. Instead, they pinned the blame on Kwan saying, "There is no question Benjamin tied up those individuals ... but Benjamin did not shoot that night."

The lone survivor, Wai Chin, was brought into the courtroom through the judge's chambers for his own security. Three plainclothes detectives surrounded him. Wai took the witness stand and explained, "That day I had nothing to do, so I go see what they had to eat." He said he knew all three men by name. Wai testified that once the three men reached the door, they "stopped, turned and with guns drawn ... the shooting began—guns firing rapidly—bullets blasting throughout with deadly accuracy." He told the jury that the only reason he survived was that he asked that the bindings not be tied so tightly, reminding the robbers "I'm an old man anyway."

George Ong, the man who found Wai outside of the club bleeding profusely, testified about what he saw. He recalled Wai telling him, "Inside is robbery and killing."

The photographs taken at the crime scene were shown to the jurors. The images were described by law enforcement as the worst they had ever encountered at a crime scene.

Chief King County Medical Examiner Dr. Donald Reay told the jury all of the victims died within "a couple of minutes" of being shot, saying the "damage was very extensive and severely incompatible with life." Dr. Reay went over six of the autopsies, while Dr. Harry Bonnell went over the remaining seven autopsies. Dr. Larry Duckert, who attended to Wai, told the court he would not have survived, had he not been able to slip out of the restraints.

An acquaintance of Benjamin's took the witness stand and countered what the defense said about a lack of any premeditation. It was his testimony he heard Benjamin and Kwan planning a robbery and speaking of the need to eliminate the witnesses.

The defense introduced a crime lab report written by a criminologist at the Washington State Patrol's crime laboratory stating there was no blood on Benjamin's clothing. Benjamin's girlfriend testified that when he returned home, he did not have any blood on his clothing. One of her friends previously told the detectives it looked to her like Benjamin's hair was wet, as though he had just showered. Another friend thought his hair looked dry but "like the wind blew it a little bit."

Michael Grubb, a firearms expert, testified on behalf of the prosecution. He explained to the jury that two .22-caliber handguns were used: a Ruger semi-automatic and a Colt revolver. He said neither of the weapons had been located. Under cross-examination, he told the court he was not positive there was more than one shooter. He did, however, say that the shell casings from the Wah Mee Club matched shell casings recovered from a house where Benjamin lived the year before. Benjamin allegedly admitted to test-firing the weapon at the house.

The trial that brought huge crowds to the courthouse each day, drew to a close. The jury was given their instructions and they filed out to begin deliberations. Less than three hours later they returned with a verdict of guilty on thirteen counts of aggravated first-degree murder and one count of first-degree assault.

During the penalty phase of the trial, the defense put Benjamin's mother on the witness stand, who told of a head injury Benjamin suffered as a child. Defense attorney Wohl also told the jury of another head injury Benjamin suffered. He blamed Benjamin's head injuries on his decision to go along with the other two men and commit the crime. A psychiatrist, Dr. Philip Lindsay, testified this type of brain injury could make a person "more gullible." Before resting his case, Wohl expounded on his belief that Benjamin never fired a gun but instead was merely present when Kwan committed the murders. The prosecution maintained that "You can't kill 13 people unintentionally."

The jury once again began deliberations but this time they bore the weight of whether Benjamin should be put to death or spend the rest of his life in prison without the possibility of parole. They chose the latter, after being unable to reach a unanimous decision on imposing the death penalty. Benjamin's family could be heard throughout the courtroom sobbing. Benjamin displayed no emotion as he was led away by the guards. As they reached the door, Benjamin turned back to take one last look at his family who had been there throughout the trial.

Following the trial, Benjamin's family paid for an advertisement in a Chinese community newspaper. The advertisement read in part:

We feel painful about Kin Ng's [Benjamin Kin Ng's] criminal behavior. It is normal for parents to love their children ... When the children grow up, they will be away from their parents and independent in society. Parents are busy with their own lives and cannot control their children ... We apologize to the families of the victims and the community.[1]

Later in a telephone interview, Benjamin's father, Yu Lai Ng, spoke about the youngest of his five children by saying:

> For 40 some years, I have been a hard worker. I never did anything bad to people. I was a barber in Hong Kong and a cook in U.S. for eight years. I had never hurt anybody in my whole life. Everybody wants their sons to be good.
>
> Benjamin did have some brain damage. When he was a boy, he always complained that he had headaches. Many times, he drank Chinese medicine to stop the headache.
>
> I have a conscience. I am sorry to the Chinese community and the victim's families. I don't have face to see anyone. Before the trial, Benjamin insisted that he did not kill anybody and told the family not to worry. Now, with all the evidence, no matter whether he shot anybody or not, he is still involved in acts against heaven.[2]

Although Kwan initially told the detectives he was responsible for killing all thirteen victims, he repudiated that statement after conferring with an attorney. He then said he left the Wah Mee Club prior to the shooting "because Ben Ng was acting strangely ... I was concerned he might shoot someone."

Kwan's trial got underway in September 1983, seven months after the shooting. He was represented by defense attorneys Don Madsen and Jim Robinson. King County Deputy Prosecutor Bill Downing once again represented the state of Washington. The jury was split evenly between men and women.

Deputy prosecutor Downing wasted no time in referring to Kwan as "a schemer, a planner," before adding, "Mak the schemer tells what he sees as being in his interest at any given time." The defense had a different take on the situation stating, "Mak the mastermind was a young immigrant man with bad associates who got tied up in the most horrible crime in the state."[3] Kwan's defense attorney blamed the shooting on an "uncharged accomplice," alluding to a fourth person.

Seattle Police Sergeant Joe Sanford told the jury that when Kwan was first questioned, he claimed he was at a bowling alley at the time the shooting occurred, before admitting, "There is no third man. I did all the shooting." Sergeant Sanford described Kwan as "visibly shaken" after being informed that one of the victims was still alive and had identified him as the shooter. "He appeared afraid, he was shaking, he lost a little of his composure. Up until that time he was a cool individual."

Defense attorney Madsen questioned if the police had advised Kwan of his rights prior to his statement. Detectives Dan Melton and Sergeant

Sanford stated Kwan was verbally advised of his rights. The defense pointed out that Wai Chin spelled the name "Mar," not "Mak." Sergeant Sanford replied, "I felt the enunciation was 'Mak.'"

Wai once again took the witness stand. Although the defense warned the jury that Wai "has a clouded memory," the panel of jurists listened intently to the lone survivor. When asked who directed the shooting, Wai replied, "I think Mak do that. He got the gun up there, he watch what his partners doing." He added Kwan was "very calm, whole time." Wai described for the jury the actual shooting by saying, "They start shooting—all three of them—bap, bap, bap." Defense attorney Robinson honed in on his previous testimony stated there were two shooters. "How many shot the guns?" Wai simply said, "All three," adding "Last time I say at least two." He was then asked, "Your position now is all three?" Wai replied without hesitation, "All three come out fire."[4]

Kwan previously told the investigators Benjamin murdered a man, but was never charged with the crime. Kwan also insisted that Benjamin previously murdered two women in Seattle but was never charged with the crime. The defense planned to put a witness on the stand who would say she saw the women alive after they were supposedly murdered and therefore Benjamin could not have killed them. However, things became complicated when the defense learned the witness had been put under hypnosis and was now telling the prosecution that she never saw the women after the date they were murdered. The defense decided against calling the witness to the stand.

They prosecution called two of Kwan's friends to the witness stand. The first friend recalled Kwan talking about robbing a gambling house in Seattle's Chinatown and murdering the witnesses. He told the court he did not take Kwan seriously even when he purchased a .22 Ruger semi-automatic. It was his testimony that Kwan lost $20,000–$30,000 in the weeks leading up to the shooting. The defense asked incredulously why he never told the police about this when they interviewed him after the murders. He stated because, "in the beginning they didn't ask."

"I don't want to do it," the next witness remembered saying, when Kwan asked him to participate in a robbery at the Wah Mee Club. Another friend of Kwan's told the jury Kwan asked him to participate in a robbery where "all the people would be killed."

The morning Kwan took the witness stand, there was a line out the door and down the hall with people hoping to get one of the seats available in the courtroom. Once he took the witness stand, Kwan stressed he left the club before any shooting took place because he became increasingly concerned that Benjamin was going to start shooting the patrons of the club. He admitted he went to the club to rough up a man but knew it would never be reported to the police. He acknowledged he concealed a .357 Magnum, but quickly said he did not intend to use the weapon unless someone else "have a gun pointed at me." Kwan emphasized he asked Benjamin and Tony to accompany him to the Wah Mee Club to "beat a guy up and tear the place down—mess up the game so they can't reopen for a while."

Kwan went on to say he and Tony entered the club first, as they had planned, followed by Benjamin a short time later. It was then, Kwan noticed, that Benjamin pulled a gun out of his bag. He also pulled a length of rope out of his bag Kwan said "he had never seen before." He said he decided to leave when he noticed a "blank look" on Benjamin's face, a look he had seen twice before. The other times, he explained, were when Benjamin shot and killed a man who was walking along the Lake Washington shore. The other time was when he shot and killed a dog. Kwan did admit the gun Benjamin used when he killed the man and the dog was one he had sold him. To explain the $5,000 the police located in his bedroom, Kwan explained his parents had given him the money in order to start his own restaurant business.

The deputy prosecutor asked Kwan, "Do you know what poker-faced is?" The man who said he was an experienced gambler, confirmed he was familiar with the expression. The prosecutor told Kwan, "A good poker player needs to be able to bluff his way through a bad hand to win." Kwan disagreed saying, "No, it takes best hand to win. When you bluffing, you don't get away with it."

A relative of Kwan's former girlfriend said she received a package from Kwan after the shootings. Inside the package was a cover letter asking that she keep the enclosed letter a secret "unless something happened to him." In the cover letter, Kwan wrote, "Peoples in Chinatown don't want me to talk. They also want to kill me." The actual letter was addressed to "dear public." The letter contained information about the shooting that occurred at the Wah Mee Club. In the letter Kwan places the blame on several business owners in Chinatown and a member of the city council he believed were involved in smuggling and dealing drugs. He blamed the police for accepting bribes to look the other way.

As the trial wrapped up, Deputy Prosecutor Downing referred to Kwan as a "cool-headed, cold-blooded young man capable of committing such an atrocity and not batting an eyelash." It took the jury two days to reach a verdict. In the end, they concluded Kwan was guilty of thirteen counts of aggravated first-degree murder and one count of first-degree assault.

During the penalty phase of the trial, Deputy Prosecutor Downing argued during his closing remarks, "This crime screams out for the death penalty." The panel of jurists agreed and recommended the death penalty for the man accused of being the mastermind behind the murders. Judge Howard formally imposed the death penalty. Kwan's defense team vowed to appeal the sentence.

Benjamin was charged with the murder of the man seen jogging along Lake Washington shore. He initially pled innocent but then changed his plea to guilty. His defense attorney explained that a trial would not change the outcome of his current life sentence. In changing his plea, Benjamin told King County Superior Court Judge Robert Elston, "On October 22, 1981, I shot a man and killed [him] with a firearm in Seward Park."

As the prosecution and the defense were busy with the trials, the police were still busy searching for the third suspect, Tony Ng. The F.B.I. placed him on their "Ten Most Wanted List," which resulted in approximately five calls a day immediately following the announcement.

As it turned out, Tony had blended into daily life in Calgary, Alberta's Chinatown. He worked at an electronics assembly plant and shared a studio apartment with a roommate. The Royal Canadian Mounted Police assisted the F.B.I. agents in what they described as a "very routine arrest." Seattle Police Lieutenant Robert Holter and Seattle Police Detective Gary Fowler were present when a pair of handcuffs was slapped on their fugitive.

A decision was made by the King County prosecution team to downgrade the charges to first-degree murder from aggravated first-degree murder. By doing so, it expediated the process of returning Tony to the United States. A treaty between the United States and Canada prevented anyone extradited from Canada to the United States from receiving the death penalty. King County Prosecutor Norm Maleng told the media:

> We have thus concluded that this is not an appropriate case in which to seek the death penalty. We have extensive evidence that Willie Mak and Benjamin Ng premeditated the robbery and murders at the Wah Mee. No such evidence exists as to Tony Ng. He was neither a participant in the planning sessions nor a partner in the other crimes, and appears to have been a last-minute recruit.[5]

It had been just over two years since thirteen people lost their lives, when Tony's trial got underway in King County Superior Court. Judge Charles Johnson took over after the defense filed an affidavit of prejudice against Judge Howard. King County Prosecutor Downing once again represented the state of Washington. Tony was represented by defense attorney Mark Mestel. An additional pool of jurors was needed due to the publicity the case had received. After a lengthy process, eleven women and one man were selected to be the jury that would decide Tony's fate.

The prosecution opened by saying Tony agreed to participate in the robbery in order to repay the $1,000 gambling debt he owed to Kwan. In Tony's statement to the police after he was arrested, he said, "If I had known that people were going to be killed or hurt, I would not have gone. Nothing is worth doing this kind of thing."

Defense attorney Mestel contended the only reason Tony went to the Wah Mee Club was because Kwan had threatened his life. Tony, he said, agreed to go along with the robbery but "was not a voluntary participant—his will was overcome by the actions of Willie Mak and Benjamin Ng."

The court spectators strained to see through the crowded courtroom as Tony approached the witness stand. Tony told the court Kwan fired a gun at his feet and threatened to kill him and his family, if he did not help with the robbery. "You're not home, I gonna kill you, kill your family, burn down restaurant, your aunt's restaurant, kill your girlfriend too. He told me not to talk to the police, they won't do anything for me."[6]

Tony stressed he did not know anything about a planned murder. "No matter what Willie gonna do to me I wouldn't have gone. I'm sorry I was there—I'm sorry." Tony told the jury he helped tie up the victims and rob them but that he left the club just as the first gunshots rang out. He did admit he accepted $4,000 for his share of the robbery proceeds. He also admitted he was present when Benjamin and Kwan tossed the two weapons into Lake Washington.

To explain why he fled the country, Tony said he "just couldn't take the pressure." He said his mother gave him $2,000 and he had the $4,000 from the robbery proceeds when he boarded a bus headed for Canada two days after the shooting. Tony admitted his mother sent him money while he was living in Calgary under the assumed name of "Jim Wong."

The prosecution pointed out Tony never told law enforcement that his life had been threatened when they questioned him after his arrest in Calgary. Tony simply stated the police never asked about anything that occurred before the trio went to the Wah Mee Club. Wai Chin testified Tony was still inside the club when the shots were fired.

During their closing arguments, the defense declared Tony was "a quiet person, a shy person ... fundamentally a decent person." The prosecution asked the jury to "close the book" on the Wah Mee Club shooting. "Today is the day of judgment for Tony Ng. You have the last word and the last word for Tony Ng is he's guilty as charged."

The prosecution and defense rested their cases and the jury filed out to begin deliberating. It took the jury almost fourteen hours over three days before they returned with a verdict that even the defense called "completely irrational." They acquitted Tony on all murder charges but convicted him of thirteen counts of robbery and one count of second-degree assault for wounding Wai Chin. In pronouncing sentence Judge Johnson said, "Mr. Ng, you played a major role before, during and after these robberies." He sentenced Tony to seven consecutive life imprisonment terms. Tony's attorneys requested a new trial but their request was denied.

Over the years, all of Benjamin and Tony's appeals were denied. Despite a 621-page appeal that Kwan's attorneys filed, the appeals court upheld the court's decision. Kwan's attorneys continued trying, filing a total of seven appeals. After almost twenty years in prison, Kwan was resentenced to thirteen consecutive life sentences.

As of 2023, Benjamin and Kwan remain in custody through the Washington Department of Corrections. Benjamin is fifty-nine years old; Kwan is sixty-two years old. Tony served twenty-eight years before being paroled. He was deported to Hong Kong upon his release from prison. Wai died ten years after being shot at the Wah Mee Club.

16
KATE MOOERS

Every year at Christmas, the governor of Washington state would issue a pardon to one or more inmates. On December 25, 1920, James Mahoney, age thirty-eight, walked out of the Walla Walla penitentiary a free man having being pardoned by Governor Louis Hart. James served two-and-a-half years of his five-to-eight-year sentence for assault and robbery.

James' conviction for grand larceny came about while he was working as a railroad brakeman. On a train ride from Missoula, Montana, to Washington state, he met Elmer Fingel who was traveling for business. Once they reached Spokane, James took Elmer to a room in the Fairmont Hotel where he allegedly gave him a drink. Elmer began to pass out and tried to leave the room but James grabbed him and choked him into unconsciousness. When Elmer woke, he discovered his $405 was missing along with his identification, letters, and clothing.

James left Spokane, but weeks later was spotted in Seattle by Elmer. Elmer returned to Spokane and notified the police. Spokane City Detective Paul Buchholz traveled to Seattle and arrested James and returned him to Spokane. James allegedly had Elmer's knife in his pocket and some of Elmer's personal belongings in his hotel room.

A trial was held in April 1918. After nineteen hours of deliberations, a jury found James guilty of assault and robbery. He was sentenced to five to eight years in prison. It was the costliest trial up to that point with a tally reaching $1,019 due to the number of witnesses summoned to testify. James lost his bid for an appeal and was taken to Walla Walla penitentiary to begin serving his term.

Three months after he walked out of prison, James married Kate Mooers, age sixty-seven. Kate was worth an estimated $200,000 (approximately $3.3 million today) in 1921 when she married James. Two months later,

Kate was missing and James was back behind bars. James was charged with first-degree forgery after allegedly signing an order giving him access to his new wife's safe deposit box. James told Seattle Police Detective Captain Charles Tennant that he and Kate separated while they were honeymooning in St. Paul, Minnesota.

An additional charge of forgery was lodged against James when the police ascertained he had allegedly forged Kate's signature on legal documents giving him power of attorney over Kate's estate.

Seattle police detectives interviewed Kate's neighbors. They relayed the last time they saw her alive was on April 16, 1921. They did recall hearing muffled screams and groans that night, but did not think anything of it at the time.

When the police were unable to locate Kate, they began a nationwide search. A witness came forward with information about a trunk that was delivered to Lake Union in the middle of April. With that information, the Seattle Police Department decided to drag Lake Union.

Defense attorney Lee Johnston represented James. When he informed his client, the police were dragging Lake Union, James adamantly denied any knowledge of a trunk. Speaking to Detective Captain Tennant's belief that James could have something to do with a trunk left on the shore of Lake Union, defense attorney Johnston told the media:

> I suppose if he's dragging for a trunk, he expects to find some evidence of some kind that will lead to the missing woman. He says the trunk was delivered on a boat in April. Doesn't say where it came from. Mahoney came to my office three weeks ago and told me he had a postcard from his wife, who was then in Havana, Cuba.[1]

Defense attorney Johnston also addressed the issue of the alleged forged legal documents. "The papers were regularly made out and are recorded in the office of the county auditor, where they should be." He expounded saying Kate made the changes of her own free will, shortly after she married James.

James' defense attorney told the reporters he sent a telegram to Kate at the Irving Hotel in New York City:

> Mahoney and she had planned to meet at the Irving early in June. I sent the wire to let her know what has happened here. She'll get it when she arrives at the Irving. We don't know where she is right now, but be assured we'll get in touch with her if we wire hard enough.[2]

Additional information was gleaned that James requested an express carrier stop by the apartment he shared with Kate late one night in mid-

April and take a trunk out to the shore of Lake Union. James allegedly rented a rowboat for one week from Howard and Sons Canoe Factory. Several people came forward reporting they saw James late at night in a rowboat on Lake Union. The witnesses reported seeing something in the rowboat, but none of the witnesses were able to determine what it was.

The police seized the rowboat for future evidence. They continued dragging Lake Union. They searched the apartment complexes and a hotel Kate owned. In checking the passenger lists for the railroad from Seattle to St. Paul, the detectives learned the couple never left for their honeymoon. James remained steadfast in his statement to the police that the couple travelled to St. Paul for their honeymoon. Once they reached their destination, James said he returned to Seattle, while his bride continued to New York to visit her sister, and then to Cuba.

Additionally, the investigators began looking for the first Mrs. Mahoney. Records indicated James married Irene Gholding Ford in St. Paul, Minnesota in 1912. Four years later, Irene filed for divorce in Seattle, but there was no record showing the divorce was finalized. The detectives learned James had power of attorney over Irene's financial affairs during their marriage.

Seattle police detectives contacted Irene's divorce attorney, C. Dell Floyd of Seattle. He did not mince words when he told the investigators Irene believed James had tried to murder her on several occasions:

> Mrs. Mahoney told me that her husband had made several attempts on her life. She wanted to make this part of the divorce complaint, but as it was difficult to prove on account of lack of witnesses, and as she had other grounds sufficient to warrant a divorce, I persuaded her to leave this phase out of her divorce papers.[3]

The first Mrs. Mahoney was located living out of state. She told the police James tried to murder her several times during their short union.

Prosecuting Attorney Malcolm Douglas told reporters he had, "established beyond a reasonable doubt" that Kate was deceased. "I regard the evidence we have secured as absolutely damning." He would not elaborate on any of the details that led him to that conclusion, but he assured the press, once the body was located, he would have further information. The King County Commissioners offered a $1,000 reward for information leading to the location of Kate's body. Kate's family added $500 to the reward.

As the police continued to drag Lake Union, defense attorney Johnston offered the following statement to the press: "Let them look. They won't find the body because it isn't there. I'm amused about this trunk episode. That can be explained when the proper time comes."

The proper time came weeks later when a trunk was found in Lake Union with the badly beaten body of Kate inside. Using the tugboat *Audrey* from the Anderson Towboat Company and three trained divers, the police discovered the trunk in an area of Lake Union. The detectives were able to determine that rope and a length of clothesline had been wrapped around the trunk and then attached to a heavy weight. Several towels had been wrapped around Kate's head. Also inside the trunk were three rugs. Each rug was stained with what appeared to be blood. There was a woman's blue coat that was missing three buttons, as well as another coat stained with what appeared to be blood, a striped house dress, a blue bathrobe, and undergarments.

A local dentist, Dr. Frank Wood, identified work he had done on Kate's teeth, thus helping to identify the body. "This unquestionably established the identity. I did the work myself."

King County Coroner Willis Corson reported the cause of death to be "blows from a blunt instrument," and noted several abrasions on Kate's head. He ascertained she had been dead for approximately three months. He noted the body had been covered with quicklime in an effort to speed up the process of decomposition.

Prior to locating the body, Prosecuting Attorney Douglas told the media he had evidence that would prove James was guilty, but he would not say what that evidence was. After the body was recovered, he told the media that when James was arrested the police located a diamond necklace in his pants pocket that belonged to Kate. The necklace was valued at $10,000. When Dr. Wood saw Kate on April 16, she was wearing the diamond necklace. When James was arrested, he was also in possession of two brooches that belonged to Kate.

"I thought you might be interested in knowing that they've found that trunk they've been looking for. I can tell you what they found in it if you want to know," a reporter told James while visiting him in jail. There was no reply, James simply turned on his heel and continued walking up and down the jail corridor.

With the discovery of the body, James was formally charged with premeditated murder. James made his first court appearance but refused to enter a plea. The judge entered a plea of innocent on his behalf. His defense counsel requested an insanity examination, but when all was said and done, the medical examiner deemed James to be sane. The defense requested a change of venue, citing that emotions were running high in Seattle. The request was denied and a trial date was set for the following month.

Days before the opening day of the trial, James' legal team hinted that they would be able to prove Kate was alive and well. In September 1921, the trial opened in King County Superior Court with Judge J. T. Ronald presiding over the proceedings. Defense attorney Louis Schwellenbach joined defense attorney Johnston. Assistant State Attorney T. H. Patterson assisted Prosecutor Douglas.

Prosecutor Douglas laid out the days leading up to the last day Kate was seen alive. He explained James visited a duplex houseboat on Lake Union and inquired about renting the vacant portion. He went on to say that James asked the owners where the deepest part of the lake was, saying he planned to do some fishing.

Days later, the prosecutor explained, James rented a white skiff and paid for a week's rental in advance. The owner of the houseboat saw the skiff tied to the houseboat on Friday evening. The next morning, James allegedly purchased 50 feet of rope and 5 pounds of lime at Buckman's Hardware Store.

That evening neighbors reported seeing James and Kate on the porch of their apartment. Prosecutor Douglas explained to the jury what happened later that night:

> Later Mr. and Mrs. Matthews saw a trunk roped and standing at the head of the stairs near the Mahoney apartment. The door was ajar. They heard hammering.
>
> There was a phone call to Seattle Transfer company that night, ordering a truck to come to (address omitted).
>
> Alvin Jorgenson, an expressman, went to that address and found a man and a trunk at the head of the stairs. He carried the trunk down and put it on the truck. The man carried a suitcase.
>
> They proceeded to the houseboat at (address omitted). *En route* they had a conversation. The man spoke of having rented the place. He said he wanted the trunk put in a boat. He said he and his partner were going to do some fishing.
>
> Jorgenson carried the trunk and put it in the boat. That boat is the same that the defendant rented from Howard.
>
> After that Saturday all was quiet in the Mahoney apartment, Sunday, Monday, Tuesday, and none of the neighbors has ever seen Mrs. Kate Mahoney alive.[4]

Prosecutor Douglas told the jury about locating the trunk after dragging Lake Union. He described the condition of Kate's body and the items in the trunk. He described the chronological events after the last time Kate was seen on April 16, 1921. He said James took a Great Northern train to St. Paul.

> Kate was not with him, because she was dead. He went to St. Paul and registered at a hotel as James E. Mahoney and wife. He wrote letters to

relatives of Mrs. Mahoney, and forged her name. He cashed some of the travelers' checks.

He returned to Seattle April 27. Filed a forged document with the county auditor, giving the defendant power of attorney over Kate's property. Then he went to a garage and got Kate's sedan and began to use it. He collected rents from her property and made several efforts to convert Kate's property into cash. He told people she was in Havana, Cuba.[5]

The four women and eight men that made up the jury listened intently to a parade of witnesses who described the last time they saw Kate alive. They heard from a bank teller who provided Kate with $460 in cashiers' checks on April 15, which she said she needed for her honeymoon. They listened as neighbors and friends told of Kate's plans to visit the East Coast during her honeymoon with James. Friends of Kate's identified the jewelry the police seized from James at the time of his arrest. They heard from the couple who rented James the houseboat and the men who rented him the skiff.

The prosecution put the express driver, Alvin Jorgenson, on the witness stand. The defense wasted no time in pointing out that although Alvin was able to remember great details about the trunk, he supposedly picked up at the Mahoney residence; he was unable to describe any of the other trunks he handled on April 16, 1921.

The jury heard from two men who worked at a tailor shop in Seattle. They both confirmed James was the man who ordered two suits and paid for them with cashiers' checks on April 18, two days after Kate was last seen alive.

The defense called a man who had known James for thirty years to the witness stand. The friend told of seeing James in Everett sometime in April. When asked, he told the court, James never mentioned being married. He recalled they talked for a bit and then James got on a train, explaining he was leaving from Everett instead of Seattle to avoid the police due to his parole status. A letter allegedly written to the friend and postmarked St. Paul, Minnesota, on April 23, 1921 was admitted into evidence. On cross-examination the friend admitted he never actually saw James get on the train, just walking towards the platform where the eastbound trains leave from.

The prosecution introduced the trunk into evidence. The jury heard from friends of Kate's who were asked to identify her body at the morgue, days after the trunk was recovered. The friends explained how they were able to identify Kate's hands despite the lime that had been used to hasten the decomposition of her body.

The jury heard from relatives of Kate's who produced letters supposedly written by Kate, but that they believed were written by James. A notary testified he did not recognize the woman James was with when he documented the change in the power of attorney early on the morning the prosecution alleged Kate was murdered.

The prosecution presented a legal document showing James signed two properties that Kate owned, over to his attorney three days after he was arrested, using the forged power of attorney.

Dr. William Dehn from the University of Washington told the court he was asked to examine the contents of Kate's stomach. He concluded there was "enough narcotics to kill 10 or 15 men."

James' sister, Delores Johnson, took the witness stand and disputed everything the other witnesses said. She told the jury her twelve-year-old daughter spent the evening with Kate and James on April 16. It was her testimony they were dancing to Irish music on Kate's phonograph until almost midnight, long after the time the express driver supposedly transported the trunk to Union Lake. She went on to explain the couple was making arrangements to leave on their honeymoon:

> On the evening of April 16 I saw Kate Mahoney at the New Baker. She came about 6 o'clock with her husband. She informed me about the rents she was leaving in our charge, the six rooms in the Denny apartments and the tenants of the Baker.
>
> We conversed about the tenants and the rents they were to pay. My daughter Margaret was there, Kate, herself, myself, her husband and my mother were in and out. They were there about an hour. She told her husband, 'Dearie, you'd better call up an expressman to get that trunk.' He went to the phone and called, and I remember him saying the trunk was going to the University district. Then they left.[6]

Delores said she spoke to Kate on the telephone on April 17:

> The next afternoon, Sunday, I talked to Kate on the phone. I phoned to her after the Spiritualist meeting. She hadn't been there. She said she had been lying down all day in the apartment. She called me up about 7 p.m. and gave me a message to give her husband when he came in.
>
> He came over and I delivered the message. He called her up and said he was on his way home. That was 9 o'clock. Then I called them both up after that and told them good-bye. That was the last time I talked to Kate Mahoney.[7]

Before Delores left the witness stand, she spoke of receiving a letter from James dated April 22, 1921 from when he was in St. Paul. In the letter

James wrote, "Kate is going on to Havana. I would sure like to go with her but can't. That is sure tough luck."

During cross-examination, Delores became increasingly frustrated and through tears, she blurted out, "He's trying to catch me lying. He asked the same question 500 times. I'm at my wits' ends [*sic*.]." Delores' twelve-year-old daughter took the witness stand and confirmed she was with Kate until almost midnight on the night of April 16.

The defense called a dentist to the stand who said there was nothing distinctive about Kate's dental work, therefore there was no way to identify her based on her dental work. A neighbor of the Mahoney's testified he saw Kate wearing the skirt that was introduced into evidence "one or two months ago." The following day, he was asked to return to the witness stand. At that time, he admitted, "It was a skirt something like that." Two physicians testified that the body in the morgue could not have been at the bottom of Lake Union based on the decomposition.

Rumors began to swirl in the city of Seattle that a man was being held in the city jail who had something to do with the Mahoney trial. The state denied knowledge of the mystery man, yet someone authorized that he be held in the jail, and the defense did not have the authority to do so. Finally, defense attorney Johnston told the press:

> The state is planning on several sensational features in Mahoney's trial. But there will be none. We know what they are planning and will circumvent them. Atkinson is being held to break Mahoney's alibi.
>
> When Mahoney was arrested, charged with forgery, he told police that Mrs. Mahoney and he had become acquainted with a Mrs. Atkinson and her son, L.D. Atkinson while on the train going to St. Paul, Minn.
>
> The Atkinsons were from London, returning via Cuba, from Honolulu. Mrs. Mahoney decided, upon their invitation, to accompany them on the trip to Havana, Cuba.[8]

Prosecutor Douglas refused to comment on the situation. Meanwhile, a detective confirmed, "Atkinson is connected with the case, yes. But you'll learn nothing until he is taken out."[9]

After Delores finished testifying, the defense team admitted the arrest of Mr. Atkinson was their doing. He explained the mystery man had swindled Delores out of money "to get witnesses for Mahoney from St. Paul." When questioned the prosecution stated, "Johnston's statement is true. But the half has not been told. Wait till [*sic*.] the Mahoney case has reached the verdict."

When it came time for closing arguments, Assistant State Attorney T. H. Patterson told the panel of jurists, "This is a serious matter. I say to you, bring in a verdict finding James E. Mahoney guilty of murder in the first degree. And shall punishment be death? Yes."

Defense attorney Schwellenbach countered with:

> I agree absolutely with one of the statements the state's attorney has just made—that this is a serious matter. When you go into the jury room you will take with you a human life. If you do what the state wants you to do, it will mean that in 30 days or so Jim Mahoney will be taken to Walla Walla, and in the early hours of the morning will be hanged.[10]

He went on to imply that the prosecution was responsible for placing the trunk into Lake Union. "Do you see what Charlie Tennant has done in this case? He has framed Jim Mahoney."

The jury began deliberating the future of James Mahoney. They returned a verdict of guilty of murder in the first degree with a recommendation for the death penalty. Upon hearing this, Delores collapsed and had to be carried from the courtroom.

Soon after, Delores was arrested and charged with forgery for allegedly being the woman purporting to be Kate in front of the notary when they changed the power of attorney. Delores pled innocent to the charge.

The mystery man, L. D. Atkinson, was released from jail at the conclusion of the trial, having never testified for either side. Days later, he was arrested and charged along with Delores with grand larceny. Mr. Atkinson made a full confession to teaming up with Delores and scamming Dora Clarke out of money he and Delores purported to need in order to repair a building. Mr. Atkinson told the authorities they used the money to pay for witnesses to assist James with his defense, including some who came all the way from St. Paul. Part of the alleged plan was also to "plant" a trunk in Lake Union for the police to find. This trunk would be filled with a liquor still and moonshine. Mr. Atkinson admitted he stood to receive $5,000 if James was acquitted.

Delores was found guilty of forgery. Things went from bad to worse for Delores when she was on the losing end of a fist fight in the county jail. This came after she referred to her fellow inmate, Lucille Brown, as a "hophead." Sheriff Starwich reported, "Dolly is a good fighter but Lucille showed more speed." Delores was seen sporting a black eye for days afterwards.

With hours left before his execution, James wrote a letter to his family. It read in part:

> Dear Mother, Sister and Margaret and Anna:
>   I got your letter of yesterday. Mr. Johnston was just here and I know the worst. Yes, Margaret, I will see the priest before I go. He was here

twice yesterday, and he is going to be with me all night tomorrow night. He will give me the last sacrament tomorrow.

Now you must be brave and forget me. My whole life has been a torture to those who love me, and even as a little boy I used to dream of dying this way, and my dream has at last come true.

When Anna comes all of you go back with her to California, or Canada, or somewhere away from Seattle–and stay together. You will never have a chance there in Seattle, and if my soul can do any good in the next world I will always be watching over you. Good-bye and God bless you all. Jimmie.

I am very glad none of you came here to see me. It would have made it harder for you and harder for me. Mr. Johnston is coming again this evening and will carry this last message to you. God bless you all. Jimmie.[11]

Delores made an eleventh-hour attempt to save her brother from the gallows. She wrote a letter confessing to being the one who murdered Kate, exonerating James from any wrongdoing, other than to help dispose of Kate's body. In Delores' letter, she wrote that she and Kate were alone in the house when a verbal altercation broke out over money she said Kate owed her:

> She got angry, and went out to the kitchen and got a butcher knife. I fought with her and got the knife. Then she ran to the front room, where her bed was, and got a revolver. I knew she kept a bar of iron in the bed, because she was afraid of burglars. I got the bar of iron and struck her over the head, so she would not shoot me. I was afraid she would kill me. When my brother came home, there I was with the dead body. He helped me dispose of it, in the manner that everyone knows of.[12]

James, who once said, "They can't do any more than hang me," walked to the gallows and was put to death early on the morning of December 1, 1922.

After many appeals and delays, Delores was sent to Walla Walla prison to begin serving a sentence of five to fifteen years for forgery, the same prison James had walked out of three months before marrying Kate. Delores was paroled after serving five years.

17

CLARENCE E. WITTE

The first sign that something was not quite right was the 1959 Oldsmobile sedan left abandoned at Sixth and Cannon Streets in Spokane in December 1959. The car was unlocked and the keys were in the ignition. The police found a wallet in the glovebox belonging to Clarence Witte, age fifty-four, of Thornton.

Spokane County Sheriff William Reilly drove out to Clarence's ranch but there was no one at home. He checked with Clarence's brother, Adam, at his farm down the road from Clarence's ranch. Adam recalled talking to Clarence in mid-December when they met on the country road but said it was not unusual for them to not see one another for periods of time.

Clarence was born on January 21, 1905, at the farmhouse where he lived at the time of his disappearance. His family had homesteaded on the property adding to their land since 1890. Clarence graduated from Thornton High School in 1924. Clarence was not married and did not have children. His relatives were not able to offer many details about his life.

Detectives James Allen and Roscoe Ghering checked Clarence's bank accounts and learned the $400,000 he kept in his accounts had not been touched since the middle of December. His ranch house sat untouched as well. They did, however, find two safes hidden under debris in an outbuilding on the property. One safe was intact, the other had been punched open. The opened safe still had some documents belonging to Clarence, as did the one that had not been opened.

Clarence was known in Whitman County as being a wealthy rancher. He owned six large ranches and usually carried $200–$300 in cash on his person (equivalent to almost $3,000 in today's money). As 1959 clicked over to 1960, there were no answers forthcoming.

On May 2, 1960, a body was pulled from the Spokane River, upriver from the Seven Mile bridge. The man's hands were bound with wire and the body was weighted down by a generator casing. It appeared the man's feet had been bound at one time based on marks left on his ankles. There were marks on his wrists indicating he had struggled to remove the wire before dying. A dentist was summoned and was able to determine the body was that of Clarence Witte.

Sheriff Reilly told reporters, "Pathologists so far can't tell us for sure whether Witte was dead when he hit the water and we've still found no one in Spokane who was familiar with what the man did here when he visited." When asked by reporters how long Clarence had been in the river, the sheriff said that had not been determined. He added, "He could have been in the water since the time he disappeared last December."

Days later, Pathologist Dr. John McCarthy determined Clarence "definitely did not drown." Sheriff Reilly reported, "Studies so far indicate that Witte definitely struggled for some time before his death." The doctor based his findings on the marks on Clarence's wrists. The pathologist was struggling to determine the cause of death due to the decomposition of the body. Tissue samples examined at the University of Washington did not provide any answers, other than to rule out any poisoning.

A funeral was held at the Methodist church in Thornton with Reverend Chester Blair officiating. Clarence was buried in the Thornton cemetery. His estate, valued at nearly $900,000 (equivalent to approximately $8,500,000 in today's money) was divided among his brother and sister. The assets included farmlands, U.S. savings bonds, his vehicle, bank deposits, the grain that was in storage, and patronage certificates.

Sheriff Reilly announced he would be taking a closer look at Clarence's vehicle due to the circumstances surrounding his death. The first thing he noticed was that Clarence had driven the car 25,000 miles in less than a year. He found two pillow cases in the car and after checking with Clarence's brother, Adam, they noticed two pillows were missing from Clarence's house. The vehicle was taken to Colfax for further examination.

Adam answered questions put to him by reporters regarding his missing brother:

> He kept to himself a great deal and we didn't think much about not seeing him until we were notified his car had been located. When I went to his house, I found a December 17 *Chronicle* in the mailbox. I believe he must have left the house the day before.[1]

Adam allowed the reporters into Clarence's house. He explained as soon as Sheriff Reilly told him they had located Clarence's car, he entered

Clarence's house and immediately noticed a pot of stew on his stove. "It looked as though he must have eaten part of it and then left the rest on the stove to keep warm. It had started to mold when I found it."[2]

Sheriff Reilly told the media, "Everywhere we turn in this case there's a puzzle." Coroner William Jones added, "it's possible that we may never be able to say positively what killed him."[3] The sheriff lamented:

> Since we don't even know what killed him, look at all the possibilities that leaves us with. For instance, we can't even say it wasn't suicide. I'll admit that's a very slim possibility. We're pretty sure he was killed and we're investigating it from that angle. But there's still the chance. We've had cases in which people were tied up tighter than Witte and we found out they did it themselves.
>
> But we haven't been able to find out any reason why he might commit suicide and we don't think he did it. It just gives you an idea of what we're up against.[4]

Sheriff Reilly continued:

> It's another instance where almost anything's possible. It could have been any spot for miles around here, including his own ranch down in Whitman County. Basing your guesses on where the car was found it would seem logical that he was killed somewhere around there and his body taken right down to the river in Peaceful Valley but he could have been killed somewhere else, and then someone drove his car up there and parked it to throw us off the track. Who knows?
>
> We'd like too, know too, how the killer or killers made Witte do what they wanted. We know he wasn't dead before they tied him up. So how did they make him comply? He was a big man, 200 pounds, close to six feet tall, good physical condition. Not too easy to manhandle. There must have been a gun or knife. Or a mickey.[5]

The calendar continued to click over year after year with none of their questions answered. Finally, on December 4, 1964, the detectives were able to ask their questions directly to the man responsible for Clarence's homicide.

Albert Donald McKinney, age fifty-one, turned himself in at the Wenatchee Police Department. Former detective, now Captain Allen, was called, along with Spokane Captain Orlan Sherrar, both of whom arrived at the police station to question Albert.

Albert admitted he murdered Clarence at his ranch on December 17, 1959. He was asked why he was at Clarence's ranch property. He said he went to Clarence's ranch after hearing other people talking about there being $1 million at the ranch. He expounded, "I didn't plan to do any murder but that's the way it turned out."

In Albert's signed confession, he admitted he lay in wait in Clarence's barn holding a gun in one hand and a club in the other. Albert explained he saw Clarence arrive home at dusk and as he crossed the ranch property, he struck him with the club. Albert admitted Clarence tried to get away, but he fired his weapon. When asked how many times he shot Clarence, Albert recalled, "two for sure—maybe three." He was asked, "you say you fired some shots at Clarence Witte when he was running. Do you know where you hit him?" Albert did not pause before answering, "I don't to this day." He did admit, "I just left him out there to bleed out, you know."

Albert spoke of placing Clarence's body in his automobile and driving to Spokane. After weighing the body down, he threw the body off a bridge near Natatorium Park. When questioned, he estimated he stole an estimated $500 in cash and valuables from Clarence's ranch. Before the interview ended, Albert said he hid the .32-caliber pistol underneath the Monroe Street bridge in Spokane, but added that when he returned for it, it was long gone.

Albert was born and raised in Oakesdale. He was a B-17 gunner for the U.S. Air Force during World War II. He flew a total of twenty-five combat missions for the United States. Between that time and his arrest, Albert worked as a ranch hand and at the Kaiser Aluminum and Chemical Company plant in Mead. At the time Albert was charged with Clarence's murder, he had been arrested for petty larceny in 1960 in Whitman County and for being drunk in public in 1959 and 1960 in Spokane.

Albert came to the attention of law enforcement for being what they had dubbed "the phantom burglar of Palouse." The phantom had been terrorizing the Palouse area for the previous four years by breaking into an estimated one hundred homes in Whitman and Spokane Counties. Although he did not steal many valuables, he made himself at home in other people's houses while they were away. The phantom was perplexing the police as he continued to break into homes, take a bath, eat the homeowner's food, and sleep in their bed while they were out of the house. He would steal small amounts of money, but leave the homeowner's valuables untouched. The phantom's most recent burglary was breaking into the headquarters of Pacific Gas Transmission Company and stealing $62.80.

It had been fifteen years since a murder trial was held in Whitman County when Albert took a seat at the defendant's table on March 3, 1965. A large crowd of spectators turned out for the trial. More than 100 people were called for jury duty. Finally, after three days, a jury was seated comprised of all male jurors. Superior Court Judge John Denoo presided over the trial. Prosecuting attorney Philip Faris represented the state of Washington. Wesley Nuxoll and Wallis Friel were appointed to represent Albert as he faced a first-degree murder charge. Despite his written confession, Albert pled innocent to the charge.

The first task at hand was to determine if Albert's confession would be admissible in the trial. The judge ordered the jury be sequestered while that issue was decided. Captains Allen and Sherrar assured the judge they had advised Albert of his rights prior to him making any statement. Captain Sherrar told Judge Denoo when they interviewed Albert four months prior, "He was easy to talk to. He talked fluently and at ease." He denied ever making threats towards the defendant or applying pressure for his answers. He said he told the defendant he would "tell the prosecutor he was cooperative." After a day of testimony, Judge Denoo ruled the confession could be admitted into evidence stating, "It is completely obvious the police did all they could to advise this man of his constitutional rights. This is not improper questioning on the part of the police. The written confession will be admitted."

Prior to the trial starting, Judge Denoo granted Prosecutor Faris' request that Clarence's body be exhumed for the purpose of a *post mortem* examination to try and determine the cause of death.

The jury listened intently as Pathologist Dr. John MacCarthy admitted he made a mistake when he failed to take an X-ray of Clarence's body during his initial examination. He explained to the jury, "It had been presumed that the victim died from exposure to the elements." Defense attorney Friel quickly questioned, "If you had considered the possibility that there was a bullet would you not have had an X-ray taken?" Dr. MacCarthy answered, "This was a mistake that we did not take an X-ray."

Under further questioning by the defense team, Dr. MacCarthy explained the only X-ray machines available were located in hospitals or clinics and he did not feel it would be "pertinent" to try and obtain an X-ray based on the advanced state of decomposition of the body that had been in the water for more than four months.

Dr. MacCarthy testified as to his original findings, which included the fact the body suffered numerous bruises and discolorations. He read his original report to the panel of jurists which included the statement, "There is no doubt that this man had struggled against his bonds for an appreciable period of time."

Dr. George Schneider, Jr., took the witness stand and explained he conducted an autopsy on the body after it was exhumed. It was at that time that he saw a bullet lodged in Clarence's shoulder, as well as a fragment of a bullet in his forearm by utilizing a whole-body X-ray. The bullet and fragment were introduced into evidence. Dr. Schneider told the court that the bullet in Clarence's shoulder "certainly could" produce death based on the trajectory. It would not be instantaneous, the doctor explained, but left unattended, it could have resulted in that outcome. When the prosecution asked Dr. Schneider if the victim was alive when the bullets entered his body, the doctor affirmed that was the case. He explained the discoloration surrounding the area, showed Clarence bled after he was shot. He told the jury, "If he bled, he had to be alive."

Clarence's brother, Adam, gave details about Clarence's life up to the time of his death. He spoke of Clarence's early years and his work operating multiple ranches. Adam recalled for the jury being told by the police they found his brother's vehicle and walking into his house for the first time since that discovery. He spoke of the layout of the ranch where Clarence had lived his entire life.

Captain Allen walked the jury through every step of the investigation beginning with the abandoned vehicle in Spokane and how he became involved after the discovery of the body in the Spokane River. He spoke at length about the autopsy while answering many questions from the defense about the procedure. Captain Allen identified the generator casing that had been attached to Clarence's body when it was recovered from the river.

A hush fell over the courtroom when Prosecutor Faris told the court, "Moreover, the evidence will show that McKinney wrote a letter describing the crime in detail—letter written shortly after it was committed. That letter didn't come into the hands of any authorities until recently." Captain Allen explained to the court when he showed the letter to Albert, he simply said, "You've got me."[6]

After Judge Denoo ruled the letter could be admitted into evidence, the prosecution called Lavinia Besola of Red Lodge, Montana, to the stand. Lavinia explained she was related to the McKinney family and she had known Albert all her life. She said they kept in contact through letters over the years. Prosecutor Faris produced the letter and asked her to identify it. Without hesitation, Lavinia positively identified the letter that was postmarked January 11, 1960, and mailed to her when she was living in Spokane. "Can you state that the letter was written in the handwriting that you had learned was the handwriting of Albert D. McKinney?" Lavinia simply said, "yes."[7]

You could hear a pin drop in the courtroom when the opening sentence of the letter was read. "It will be four weeks this coming Thursday since I murdered that guy and they haven't come for me yet." In the letter Albert allegedly wrote, he "whittled out a good club that day" from wood located on Clarence's property while waiting for him to return home. Writing about the murder, he described, "I shot left-handed and missed—I changed the gun to my right hand and let him have it twice." In the letter, he wrote Clarence yelled, "Oh, please don't!"[8]

Other excerpts of the letter mentioned burning the club in the woodstove in the house, preparing a meal, and rifling a safe in Clarence's garage. Albert allegedly wrote, "I tried to carry him to the car but he was too heavy and limber so I decided to wait until rigor mortis set in." Once he managed to get Clarence's body into the vehicle, he wrote, "I got to drive a real car anyway before my exit." In the letter he described dumping the body in the Spokane River. He also allegedly wrote, "I probably should have stayed around a day and looked for more loot." At one point towards the end of the letter, Albert allegedly wrote, "I want you to just see how little I care to live any longer."[9]

A former employer of Albert's took the witness stand for the defense and described Albert as an honest, hard-working employee. He told the jury Albert had worked in his apple orchards the past few years, adding, "he was a real good worker." As he stepped down from the witness stand, he stopped and shook hands with Albert.

A psychiatrist, Dr. Rob Kinney, told the jurists that although Albert was not insane, he suffered from a "maladjusted personality." The doctor blamed Albert's experience in World War II on the disorder.

Next the defense called a local tavern owner who testified Albert never caused any problems in his establishment. "He wouldn't argue with anybody." He added, "As the years progressed, he became more morose and sadder—he seemed withdrawn." He also blamed the change on Albert's time in the military. Albert's brother also testified to the change in personality he witnessed over time.

Finally, it was time for the jury to begin deliberations. Judge Denoo reminded them they were to "draw no inference of guilt from his silence," referring to Albert not taking the witness stand in his own defense. The judge explained they were to decide between first-degree murder, second-degree murder, or innocent. If, he explained, they returned a verdict of guilty of first-degree murder, they also had to decide if the death penalty was warranted.

Less than six hours later, the jury announced they had reached a verdict. Albert displayed no outward emotions when learning the jury found him guilty of first-degree murder. They did not, however, recommend the death penalty. The "Phantom of the Palouse" was sentenced to life imprisonment.

10

MYSTERIES

Jennifer Bedingfield

"She was the star, the angel," were the words used to describe Jennifer Bedingfield, age fourteen. On May 8, 1999, Jennifer and her father, Lance, were riding their bikes across Benson Highway at SE 224th Street at approximately 9:40 p.m. when a car struck Jennifer. The car that struck her did not stop. Jennifer died at the scene of the accident from massive head injuries. Her father was not injured.

Jennifer and her father had ridden their bikes to a convenience store near their home in Kent for a last-minute Mother's Day gift. They had been riding on the highway sidewalk when they crossed the northbound lanes just south of the Southeast 224th Street. They waited in the center lane for traffic to clear when a car traveling north, straddling its lane and the center lane, struck Jennifer. Witnesses told the investigators the car appeared to slow down but then kept going. There were no skid marks to indicate the car attempted to stop. Washington State Patrol spokesperson Tom Foster told reporter Stacey Burns of *The News Tribune*, "It doesn't appear he ever saw the individual. They were in a real bad spot."

Jennifer enjoyed spending time with her family and friends. Her family owned the Alpine German Deli and Restaurant in Fife where Jennifer helped by working as a hostess. Jennifer liked helping her grandmother in her garden and playing with her grandparent's dogs. She enjoyed playing basketball at school and playing darts at the family restaurant. Jennifer had a trip planned to Arizona with her maternal grandparents during her upcoming summer vacation. The following summer, she planned to travel to Germany with her paternal grandmother.

Upon learning their classmate had been killed, Jennifer's friends made a memorial for her at her school, Kent Junior High School. A homemade sign read: "Jennifer Bedingfield—We Want Jennifer Back!" Her classmates placed her desk and bouquets of flowers around the school's flagpole. They placed her lunchtime favorites—an order of nachos and a can of soda—on top of the desk. Next to the desk, Jennifer's classmates wrote messages to her on index cards and hung the cards on a poster outlined in blue tissue paper. One card read, "To the girl with a heart, to the girl with a soul. We all love you. We all miss you. Now you are home." Another card read, "You were such a good friend and will remain in my heart." Jennifer's teachers and classmates wore carnations with a label that read, "In loving memory of Jennifer Bedingfield. January 31, 1985–May 8, 1999."

The Washington State Patrol described the car that struck Jennifer as a 1980–1982 blue Datsun 310 passenger car. The vehicle was found abandoned in Enumclaw. Initially the investigators received several hundred tips, but none of the tips led them to the driver of the vehicle that killed Jennifer. The years clicked by but there were no answers. The Washington State Patrol Cold Case Team is actively working the case and is asking the public to come forward with any information. They can be reached at 425-401-7740. Please reference case #99-004221.

Brian Eugene Helmuth

Right now we know very little about him. If he decided to head off to Washington State, it's certainly his prerogative as an adult human being. Even if we did find him, we would basically say, "Hey, your parents are worried about you. Give them a call."

Those were the words Washington State Patrol Detective Sergeant Rob Reichert said in regards to missing person Brian Eugene Helmuth in July 1999.

Brian was born on August 10, 1960. When he was last seen, he weighed approximately 285 pounds and was 5 feet 11 inches tall. He had brown hair, hazel eyes, and a full mustache and beard. He had a "V" scar on the back of his hand that was 2–3 inches wide.

In 1999, Brian worked for the University of Alaska Anchorage and lived with his parents in Wasilla, Alaska. On June 14, 1999, Brian phoned his parents after work and said he was going to a movie in the late afternoon. That was the last time his parents ever heard from Brian.

His parents contacted the Alaska State Troopers and filed a missing persons report. They followed Brian's credit card trail and learned he took a flight on Reno Air from Anchorage to Seattle. He checked into the Motel 6 in Bremerton at 3 a.m. on June 15, 1999. At 11:15 p.m. that same day, he checked out of the motel.

On June 16, 1999, at 1:30 a.m. three people boarded the passenger ferry *Tyee* in Bremerton. When the ferry reached Seattle, only two people departed. There was no sign of the third passenger.

The ferry retraced its route and was joined by the U.S. Coast Guard. They used a lifeboat and helicopter but did not find Brian or his luggage. The other passengers were able to give the police a description of the man they remembered seeing on the ferry who was carrying a piece of luggage.

When the police searched their records, they saw similarities with Brian's missing person flyer out of Alaska. The Alaska State Troopers faxed a photograph of Brian. The police showed the photograph to four members of the crew of the ferry. All four crew members believed the man they saw looked similar to the man on the missing person's flyer, but they could not be 100 percent positive. The hotel clerk at Motel 6 was not able to positively identify the man who checked into the motel.

Detective Sergeant Reichert told Ed Friedrich of the *Kitsap Sun*, "There's always going to be questions of did he jump off the boat or find some scheme to get off the boat? Maybe he's trying to cover up he is alive. We'll never know 100 percent on that."

Two decades later, neither the Alaska State Troopers or the Washington State Patrol have any answers. No one has ever seen or heard from Brian since June 14, 1999. The Washington State Patrol's Cold Case Team would appreciate any information. They can be reached at 425-401-7740 and reference case #99-005635. Alternatively, the Alaska State Troopers Missing Persons Clearinghouse can be reached at 907-269-5058 and reference case 99-39372.

James Dinh

Washington State Patrol was called to a car crash on northbound Interstate 5 near 272nd Street in Kent, on November 1, 1998, at about 5 p.m. They learned a white Volvo station wagon attempted to merge onto Interstate 5 southbound lanes from the shoulder. A Volkswagen Scirocco swerved to avoid the Volvo but collided with a pickup truck that in turn hit a Mitsubishi Montero occupied by a family of five.

The Mitsubishi Montero flipped across the freeway median and landed on its roof in the southbound lane. A Greyhound bus was traveling in the southbound lane and was not able to stop in time. The Greyhound bus collided with the Mitsubishi Montero. The crash caused James Dinh, age two to be ejected from the family car. The family was rushed to Harborview Medical Center in Seattle. James succumbed to his multiple injuries. The rest of the family, James' parents, his one-year-old sister, and an extended member of the family suffered injuries in the crash.

The driver of the white Volvo never stopped. The Volvo was described as a "boxy-looking station wagon." The driver was described as a heavy-set white male who wore glasses. The white Volvo had green and white license plates. More than two decades have passed since the car crash. The Washington State Patrol is asking that if anyone has any information to please contact their Cold Case Team at 425-401-7740 and reference case #98-012573.

Edward Reece

The rain was coming down on the evening of November 23, 1998. At approximately 5:30 p.m. a car was driving westbound on SR 900 near South 129th Street. When the driver changed lanes, he did not see a pedestrian. The driver struck Edward Reece, who was crossing the road. The driver stopped to help Edward, as did another pedestrian. As they were rendering aid to Edward, another car drove through the accident scene, striking and killing Edward. That driver failed to stop at the crime scene.

The vehicle that fled the scene of the crime was described as being one of three styles of vehicle. Witnesses believed it was either a dark-colored older "boxier" Honda Accord type hatchback with "pop-up" headlights or a beige, tan, or cream-colored Mazda 323, 326, or it could have been a Toyota.

The Washington State Patrol is asking for assistance in locating the driver who fled the scene of the crime. If you have any information, please call their Cold Case Team at 425-401-7740 and reference case #98-013411.

Peter Duane Schryver

Peter Schryver was riding his motorcycle on SR 509 near 4th Avenue South in Federal Way on September 1, 1990. As he entered a curve, he lost control of his motorcycle and crashed. A vehicle struck Peter and fled the scene of the crime. Peter was rushed to Harborview Hospital in Seattle but died shortly thereafter.

Peter was born in Olympia on June 28, 1967. He graduated from Timberline High School in 1985 then attended South Puget Sound

Community College. He had been married for one year at the time of his death. He was working as an auto mechanic when the accident occurred.

Witnesses at the scene of the accident described seeing a brown or olive-colored Jeep CJ stop for a moment, before leaving the scene of the crime. The witnesses believed the Jeep CJ was from the late 1970s to early 1980s.

The Washington State Patrol is asking the public to come forward with information before any more time goes by. Their Cold Case Team can be reached at 425-401-7740 and reference #90-020601992.

Judy Tilden

When a motorcycle crashed at 2:30 in the morning on January 22, 1995, Judy Tilden rushed to help the injured motorcyclist on northbound I-405 at Northeast 85th Street. As Judy was providing aid, a vehicle drove through the traffic collision killing Judy. The car that hit Judy never stopped.

Witnesses believed the vehicle was a large tan or white Ford. The license plate may have contained the numbers 721. If you have any information, please contact the Washington State Patrol Cold Case Team at 425-401-7740 and reference Case #95-001234.

Toni Ann Tedder

Toni was born on July 25, 1972, in Tacoma. Her father was in the U.S. Air Force so her early years were spent in Germany, Fort Ord, California, and Orofino, Idaho. The family moved to Clarkston in 1983.

Toni excelled at academics and sports while in high school and was known for being very outgoing. She was active on the drill team, track and cross country, the Select Six choir group, and band. Toni graduated from Clarkston High School in 1990. On July 25, 1990, Toni turned eighteen years old. Three days after her birthday, she was stabbed to death at approximately 5 a.m. while sleeping on a couch in her family's living room.

Toni's sister was awoken by an intruder in the house. Toni's sister described the intruder as a white male in his twenties, 5 feet 9 inches, medium build, blue eyes, and dark brown wavy hair. He was wearing a shirt, blue jeans, and tennis shoes.

The police arrived and began their investigation. They believed the intruder entered the two-story home through either an unlocked door or window. The detectives located a wooden-handled fishing fillet type knife with a 6-inch blade that they suspected was the murder weapon. A police sketch was created based on the information Toni's sister provided of the assailant.

The Clarkston Police Department worked with the Washington State Patrol, Asotin County Sheriff's Department, Lewiston Police Department, Seattle Police Department, and the F.B.I. The University of Washington medical and psychological units tried to develop a personality profile of the killer. The personality profile indicated the murderer was young, in his twenties, either lived in the neighborhood, or was familiar with the area.

They submitted their information to the Washington State Homicide Information Tracking System as well as the F.B.I.'s Violent Criminal Apprehension Program for comparison to similar crimes in the United States. They did not receive any leads, but by the end of the year, the investigators had eliminated 100 potential suspects. There was one suspect that looked like the police sketch that they could not eliminate.

In 1994, the police reopened the case based on new information they received. They were concentrating on one suspect. Clarkston Police Detective Sergeant Ronald Roberts told the Associated Press, "We're looking at one suspect, if not more, that we developed from information we received from the public. We're still confident this will be resolved sooner or later. The person who did this can't live with this forever." He did indicate they collected unidentified fingerprints at the crime scene, as well as other evidence. He said the one previous suspect was cleared.

At the one-year anniversary of the murder, Clarkston Chief of Police Michael Erp told the media "This is not the kind of crime that is solved easily." Three decades later, his words still ring true. Toni's parents have passed but the rest of her family is still waiting for answers. The Washington State Patrol Cold Case Team asks that if anyone has any information to please call them at 425-401-7740 and reference case #WSP90-000001 or contact the Clarkston Police Department at 509-758-1680.

Helen Doe

The first phone call came in at 2:48 on Tuesday, May 14, 1991. The frantic caller reported that two trucks had crashed, resulting in a huge fire on Interstate 5 near Kalama.

The Washington State Patrol arrived on scene within minutes to find a tractor trailer and a semi-truck completely engulfed in a gigantic fireball. They were able to determine that the tractor-trailer rear-ended a semi-truck. Kalama Fire Chief Richard Merz told reporter Pauline Bains of the *Longview Daily News,* "The way the two trucks were put together and rammed into each other, at first it looked like one tractor and two trailers."

He said that upon arrival at least 90 percent of the trucks were engulfed in flames.

Donald Pearl, age fifty-six, of Salem, Oregon, was driving the semi-truck for Boise Cascade Corporation. He suffered injuries but was able to tell reporter Pauline Bains, "They hit me hard. To get that far up inside the trailer, they had to hit hard." He explained that upon impact his head went forward and came back with enough force to break the rear window of the cab of his truck. He said he detached the cab from the trailer in the hopes it would not catch on fire.

Donald described the traffic scene just prior to the collision. He said traffic had slowed to a few miles per hour due to road construction. He went onto say he began braking before the Kalama River exit when the tractor-trailer crashed into his semi-truck. The force, he said, pushed the tractor-trailer approximately thirty-feet into his truck.

The driver of the tractor-trailer died in the fire. He was identified as Lester Dean Harvel, age twenty-six. He was from New Haven, Michigan, and was driving for TLC Lines, Incorporated out of St. Clair, Missouri. The investigators learned there was a female passenger. Their investigation showed she did not work for the TLC Lines.

Traffic was rerouted for ten hours before Interstate 5 completely reopened. Hours later, some of the newsprint from the Boise Cascade truck that was left in the road median reignited. The firefighters were able to quickly extinguish the fire.

A special team of investigators from the Bellevue office of the Washington State Patrol were called to the scene to try and determine the cause of the accident. Detective Scott Cartier told the media that the initial cause of the investigation was "just flat inattention." Their work identifying the female who perished in the fire proved to be a challenge. She was given the name of Helen Doe, instead of the usual Jane Doe, due to the proximity to Mount St. Helens. She was buried in an unmarked grave at the Longview Memorial Park and Cemetery.

The investigators were able to trace Lester's route by gas receipts from Missouri through Kansas, Colorado, Wyoming, Utah, Idaho, and Oregon before he unloaded freight in Tacoma. Detectives were trying to determine when and where the female joined Lester. The trucking company did not have a record of an authorized passenger leading the investigators to believe the female may have been hitchhiking.

The autopsy of the unidentified female revealed she was probably in her twenties and approximately 5 feet 1 inch to 5 feet 4 inches with a slender build and weighed between 110 and 130 pounds. She had a slight gap between her lower middle teeth. She was of Native American decent. She had long brown hair, high cheekbones, and a dark complexion. Witnesses who saw her prior to the crash said she was wearing Levi jeans, a grey shirt, a black cowboy vest, and feather earrings. She had severe scoliosis with a convexity to the right. The investigators tried to determine her identity through dental records, but were not successful.

The years went by but no answers were forthcoming as to the female's identity. The start of a new century brought advanced technology to law enforcement. In 2014, Helen Doe had still not been identified. A decision was made to exhume her body in order to obtain a DNA sample. The Cowlitz County Coroner's Office and the Washington State Patrol exhumed the body on January 8, 2014.

Due to the possibility Helen Doe was of Native American decent, members of the Puyallup tribe gave her burial site a blessing and placed gifts of beads and symbolic items with her remains.

The D.N.A. sample was sent to the University of North Texas for possible identification. Her bones were removed from the metal casket and sent to a forensic anthropologist in Seattle. The anthropologist agreed to do a facial reconstruction in an attempt to show what Helen Doe may have looked like.

Washington State Forensic Anthropologist Dr. Kathy Thompson completed the reconstruction of the female's skull. Forensic artist Natalie Murry created a drawing of what the victim may have looked like when she was alive. Despite their best efforts, no one came forward with information as to her identity. In 2014, Cowlitz County Coroner Tim Davidson told reporter Barbara LaBoe with the *Longview Daily News* "I want to make sure she gets back to her family. So they can have some closure after wondering what's happened to her for all these years." Washington State Patrol Detective Greg Wilcoxson added, "It's a big step. We're going to keep working on it. It might not happen today, but we'll have everything on file and we're going to just keep our fingers crossed."

Years later, the Washington State Patrol is still waiting for an answer. Thirty years after the crash that took her life, detectives are asking for the public's help in identifying their Helen Doe. In 2022, forensic artist Natalie Murry released an updated sketch as to what Helen Doe may have looked like when she was alive. Anyone with information can contact the Washington State Patrol Cold Case Team at 425-401-7740 and reference case #00-004956.

Precious Jane Doe

This young girl was precious to me because her moral decision from her proper upbringing cost her, her life. I knew she had to be precious to her family too, so I had to find them. We needed to give her name back to her and return her remains to her family.

This is what Snohomish County Detective Jim Scharf told reporters when questioned about an unidentified female.

The case began on August 14, 1977, when a group of people looking for blackberries near Silver Lake in Everett came across the body of a female. Her body was in the advanced stages of decomposition but the detectives who responded to the crime scene could tell she had been shot in the head seven times. The female victim was wearing a striped tank top, cut-off denim shorts, and blue-and-white Mr. Sneekers shoes. She had seventeen cents in her pocket but no identification, leaving the police with a mystery on their hands.

Days later, Officer Roy Reed with the Seattle Police Department spoke to a man who informed him a friend of his, David Roth, claimed to have recently murdered a hitchhiker. Officer Reed contacted a sheriff's detective, Kenneth Sedy.

The police were familiar with David, having just arrested him days before. The police were called after David was seen with a gun at a park outside of Gold Bar. The police seized a .22-caliber rifle and some marijuana from his vehicle. They impounded the vehicle. David was released from jail after a couple of days.

The police searched David's car and located shell casings, peacock feathers, and bungee cords. Ballistics tests showed the bullets in the female's skull matched David's weapon.

On January 18, 1979, police questioned David about the unidentified female. He quickly confessed to the murder. A jury convicted David of first-degree murder.

When David entered prison, the female still had not been identified and became another Jane Doe. The detectives had sent her hands to the F.B.I. Laboratory in the hopes of identifying her but she was not in their system. The police released a sketch of what she may have looked like, but no one came forward with any information. A forensic dentist was able to determine the victim had had dental work done. A search of dental records did not produce any results.

Thirteen years after the body was found, a forensic artist, Detective John Hinds, used a plaster cast from what remained of her skull. Photographs were taken and flyers were circulated across the country, but there were no replies.

Years went by and a decision was made to exhume the female's body from her resting place in the sunrise section of the Cypress Memorial Park. A court order was granted and her body was exhumed and a D.N.A. sample was obtained. Scientists and anthropologists were able to determine her age to be between fifteen and twenty-one years of age. Her D.N.A. was not in any database and she remained a Jane Doe.

David was released from prison in 2005 after serving twenty-six years. Detectives asked for his help in creating a new sketch. He was surprised that anyone was still attempting to identify his victim. He agreed to assist the detectives. He explained that he never knew her name but he did provide a few details about her features. He told the detectives she was hitchhiking and he gave her a ride. When she refused to have sex with him, he strangled her and shot her in the head. Despite their best efforts, there were no answers forthcoming as to the identity of Jane Doe.

More than four decades passed before Jane Doe's identity was finally known. Technology had improved over time and detectives used genetic genealogy to create a family tree for the unidentified female. They located a biological half-brother of their Jane Doe. They were finally able to put a name to their victim. She was identified as Elizabeth "Lisa" Ann Elder. Lisa was born in Hood River, Oregon, in 1959 and adopted when she was two years old. Elizabeth was eighteen years old when she was reported as a runaway. Two weeks later, she was murdered. Lisa was given a proper burial in her family's plot and the mystery came to a close.

19
MISDEMEANORS

A law enacted in Washington state in 1909 prohibited all slot machines or other gambling devices. If found guilty of this gross misdemeanor, a fine of $1,000 and a year in a county jail could be imposed. That law increased to a felony in 1937 with the exception of gambling devices in private clubs. If an operator was found to be playing with cards or dice, they could face up to five years in prison.

A law placed on the books in 1933 made it a misdemeanor to take any flowers, shrubs, or plants from any state-owned land or any land within 300 feet of the center line of a state highway or county road in Washington state.

In 1941, Washington state Governor Langlie issued a proclamation declaring twenty areas in Washington state as "protective defense areas" for the purpose of national defense. It was a gross misdemeanor to operate a camera, telescope, or binoculars within the protected area or the air above or the land surrounding the protected area. Carrying a firearm, ammunition, or explosives of any kind was also prohibited in the protected areas. Examples of the protected areas included Kitsap County, Bainbridge Island Naval Station, Bremerton shipyards, Jefferson County, Oyster Bay, Sand Point Naval Station, King County, Fort Lewis, Pierce County, and the Seattle Federal Building.

Not showing your gasoline ration book during World War II was considered a violation of war-time law, a federal misdemeanor.

During World War II, a jury convicted Saul Freeman and Irving Rose of a misdemeanor for violating the rationing laws. Saul was convicted of buying forty quarters of beef without using his ration points and then selling Irving eleven quarters of the beef without taking his ration points. Together, they purchased eight barrels of meat and cheese without using their ration points.

In 1949, an owner of a building where gambling took place, and any person caught gambling, could be convicted of a misdemeanor and sentenced to one year in a county jail. The operator of a gambling establishment could face a felony charge and spend five years in prison.

In 1953, it became a misdemeanor to serve a parolee an alcoholic drink. Additionally, parolees were not allowed to work anywhere where alcohol was served.

In 1955, it became a misdemeanor for a motorist to pick up a hitchhiker. This came about after a driver was carjacked by two armed men near Ephrata. That same year, a man took his daughter for a walk in Spokane but soon faced a misdemeanor charge of picking wildflowers along the road.

Thomas Maloney surrendered to the authorities in 1956 after being indicted by a grand jury with four misdemeanors and a felony relating to charges of vice and corruption. He was well known in Seattle and Spokane for operating illegal gambling houses and horse tracks.

Ronald Morgan was released from jail in 1959 for passing bad checks. In sentencing him, the judge cut him a break by only charging him with a misdemeanor, even though the checks he wrote were for more than $25. He had not been out of jail very long before writing seven more bad checks. He kept each check below $25, thereby keeping the charge a misdemeanor. His defense attorney, Wallace Cavanagh, commented that Ronald's IQ was 147, saying, "No wonder he learned so quickly," referring to keeping the checks below the $25 threshold.

In the 1950s, committing a gross misdemeanor while on duty could have earned a firefighter at Coulee Dam Fire Department the much-dreaded Bonehead Cup. Previous misdemeanors included blocking a fire truck, going the wrong direction, or not knowing how to use a piece of apparatus. Also in that decade, hotels were required to maintain a record of all hotel guests for one year or face a misdemeanor charge. This law was aimed at lessening prostitution.

Beginning in the 1950s, it was a misdemeanor to place additional coins in the parking meter to extend the time past the allotted one hour. Only pennies and nickels were allowed; dimes were not accepted.

Long before there were cell phones, there were private landlines. Before that, there were party lines for those who wanted to save money. A party line was used by multiple people. It was a misdemeanor to not hang up the phone when someone needed to use the telephone to call for emergency services.

ENDNOTES

Chapter 1

1 *The Columbian*, July 12, 1965, p. 15.
2 *The Tacoma News Tribune*, June 10, 1981, p. 1.
3 *Ibid.*
4 *Ibid.*
5 *The News Tribune*, June 11, 1981, p. 3.
6 *Ibid.*
7 *Ibid.*

Chapter 2

1 *The News Tribune*, August 23, 1929, p. 24.
2 *The Tacoma Daily Ledger,* May 7, 1910, p. 14.
3 *Ibid.*
4 *Ibid.*
5 *Ibid.*
6 *Ibid.*
7 *The News Tribune*, February 23, 1969, p. 117.

Chapter 3

1 *The Columbian*, May 14, 1965, p. 1.
2 *The Columbian*, May 26, 1965, p. 1.
3 *Ibid.*
4 *The Columbian*, June 14, 1965, p. 2.
5 *Ibid.*
6 *The Columbian*, July 28, 1967, p. 20.

Chapter 4

1 *The News Tribune*, December 6, 1974, p. 3.
2 *Ibid.*
3 *Spokane Daily Chronicle*, October 17, 1978, p. 1.

Chapter 5

1   *The Columbian*, July 29, 1948, p. 2.

Chapter 6

1   *The News Tribune*, September 26, 1907, p. 2.
2   *The Tacoma Daily Ledger*, November 17, 1907, p. 1.
3   *Ibid.*
4   *The Tacoma Daily Ledger*, November 26, 1907, p. 1.
5   *Aberdeen Herald*, November 28, 1907, p. 1.
6   *Aberdeen Herald*, December 2, 1907, p. 1.

Chapter 7

1   *Longview Daily News*, July 2, 1952, p. 17.

Chapter 8

1   Wilson, L., *Longview Daily News*, May 17, 1985, p. 1.
2   *Longview Daily News*, November 25, 1996, p. 2.
3   *Longview Daily News*, February 26, 1999, p. 1.
4   Smith, L., *Longview Daily News*, March 6, 1999, p. 2.

Chapter 9

1   *The Columbian*, March 27, 1950, p. 1.
2   *The Columbian*, June 28, 1950, p. 1.
3   *The Columbian*, June 28, 1950, p. 4.
4   *Ibid.*
5   *Spokane Daily Chronicle*, November 28, 1950, p. 41.
6   *The Columbian*, May 11, 1951, p. 1.
7   *Longview Daily News*, January 2, 1953, p. 1.
8   *The Tacoma News Tribune*, January 4, 1953, p. 2.
9   *Ibid.*

Chapter 10

1   *The Seattle Star*, May 21, 1934, p. 14.
2   *The Seattle Star*, August 14, 1934, p. 12.
3   *The Seattle Star*, October 22, 1934, p. 14.
4   *Ibid.*
5   *Ibid.*
6   *The Seattle Star*, October 24, 1934, p. 2.
7   *Ibid.*
8   *Spokane Daily Chronicle*, February 25, 1931, p. 1.

Chapter 11

1 *The Spokesman-Review*, December 7, 1928, p. 1.
2 *Spokane Daily Chronicle*, December 10, 1928, pp. 2, 11.
3 *Spokane Daily Chronicle*, December 13, 1928, p. 18.
4 *Ibid.*
5 *Ibid.*
6 *Ibid.*
7 *Ibid.*
8 *Ibid.*

Chapter 12

1 *Detroit Free Press*, April 13, 1961, p. 3.
2 *The Holland Evening Sentinel*, July 26, 1961, p. 22.
3 *Detroit Free Press*, April 30, 1966, p. 3.

Chapter 13

1 *Spokane Daily Chronicle*, April 17, 1976, p. 1.
2 *Spokane Daily Chronicle*, June 3, 1976, p. 1.

Chapter 14

1 *The Spokesman-Review*, November 18, 1959, p. 13.
2 *The Columbian*, May 12, 1960, pp. 1, 2.
3 *The Columbian*, May 13, 1960, p. 2.
4 *Ibid.*

Chapter 15

1 *The Olympian*, September 2, 1983, p. 12.
2 *Ibid.*
3 *Spokane Daily Chronicle*, September 21, 1983, p. 20.
4 *Spokane Daily Chronicle*, September 23, 1983, p. 11.
5 *The Spokesman-Review*, October 17, 1984, p. 23.
6 *The Bellingham Herald*, April 13, 1985, p. 10.

Chapter 16

1 *The Seattle Star*, May 26, 1921, p. 4.
2 *Ibid.*
3 *The Spokesman-Review*, May 29, 1921, p. 3.
4 *The Seattle Star*, September 22, 1921, p. 14.
5 *Ibid.*
6 *The Seattle Star*, September 29, 1921, pp. 1, 7.
7 *Ibid.*
8 *Ibid.*
9 *Ibid.*

10　*The Seattle Star*, October 1, 1921, p. 1.
11　*The Seattle Star*, December 1, 1922, p. 17.
12　*Ibid.*

Chapter 17

1　*Spokane Chronicle*, May 6, 1960.
2　*Ibid.*
3　*The Spokesman-Review*, May 29, 1960, p. 11.
4　*Ibid.*
5　*Ibid.*
6　*Spokane Daily Chronicle*, March 9, 1965, p. 9.
7　*Ibid.*
8　*Ibid.*
9　*Ibid.*

BIBLIOGRAPHY

The Tacoma Daily Ledger (November 17, 1907)

Aberdeen Herald (November 28, 1907)

The Spokesman-Review (May 29, 1921, December 7, 1928, November 18, 1959, October 17, 1984)

Spokane Daily Chronicle (December 10, 1928, December 13, 1928, February 25, 1931, November 28, 1950, March 9, 1965, April 17, 1976, June 3, 1976, October 17, 1978, September 21, 1983, September 23, 1983)

The News Tribune (September 26, 1907, August 23, 1929, February 23, 1969, December 6, 1974, June 11, 1981)

The Columbian (July 29, 1948, March 27, 1950, June 28, 1950, May 11, 1951, May 12, 1960, May 13, 1960, May 14, 1965, May 26, 1965, June 14, 1965, July 12, 1965, July 28, 1967)

Longview Daily News (July 2, 1952, January 2, 1953, November 25, 1996, February 26, 1999)

The Holland Evening Sentinel (July 26, 1961)

Detroit Free Press (April 13, 1961, April 30, 1966)

The Olympian (September 2, 1983)

The Bellingham Herald (April 13, 1985)

Wilson, L., *Longview Daily News* (May 17, 1985)

Smith, L., *Longview Daily News* (March 6, 1999)

The Tacoma News Tribune (May 7, 1910, January 4, 1953, June 10, 1981)

The Seattle Star (May 26, 1921, September 22, 1921, October 1, 1921, December 1, 1922, May 21, 1934, August 14, 1934, October 22, 1934, October 24, 1934)